Tantra Sā

A practical introduction to Kaula Magick

By Mogg Morgan
(Sahajanāth)

Mandrake

The five pain bearing obstacles
the root cause of trouble and strife
Ignorance, Ego, Revulsion, Attachment
and Clinging to life.

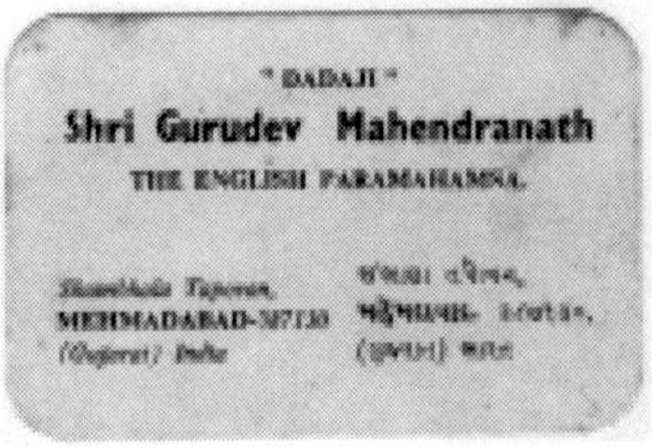

(1911 - 1988)

Tantra Sādhana 3

First Edition

Contents

Guide to Pronounciation

Several different conventions are commonly used to render unfamiliar Sanskrit sounds. The situation is complicated by the fact that academic practice has changed over time and many older books adopt different conventions. It has to be said that the older methods are useful, especially as the more modern transcriptions make use of diacritical marks not normally available on ordinary typewriters or indeed at the typesetters. To get you started:

a as in put and long ā as in father.
i as in fit and long i as in fee.
u as in put and long ū as in boo.
ṛ as in p*ur*dy.
k as in kill.
c as in chill.
p as in pill.
ṭ as in try (retroflex).
t as in french 'tout' (dental).
ṣa and a as in ship.

This rough guide may usefully be supplemented by a study of standard handbooks. It is not necessary to learn Sanskrit, but reading of the first chapter of something like *Teach Yourself Sanskrit* by Michael Coulson, might help with unfamiliar words.

Preface

Murugan was a Tamil Guru of absolute integrity and honesty, great and critical knowledge and a very kind heart.

"Who was your Guru?" I asked.

He thought about the question for a moment. "My teacher and his teacher before him, and before that all belonged to the line of Yakkupo."

Back then my knowledge of Tamil was rudimentary and the name meant very little to me. I nodded inanely.

"You have never heard of this person?"

I had to admit that I had not.

"Then," he said, "let me translate that into English. Yakkupo is not a Tamil name. What I am saying is that the Siddhas of my tradition come from the line of Jacob. Now do you understand?"

I wasn't sure. Could Murugan be talking about a character from the Bible?

"The only Jacob I know about," I said, "is from the Old Testament."

"Precisely!" he interrupted, "and what do you know about this Jacob?"

I thought for a moment. It had been a long time since I read the Bible. "Jacob was a patriarch of the Hebrews before they became the nation of Israel."

"Yes."

"Urr," I was stumbling for something relevant to say. Then something I learnt at Sunday school popped into my head, "Jacob", I said rather lamely, "blessed the Pharaoh."[1] "He was the father of Joseph who during a long period of famine settled his people to Egypt. That the Egyptians could shelter these ancient victims of a great famine is a fact overshadowed by the later accounts of the eventual servitude of the Jews as told in the story of the Exodus. At the end of the *Book of Genesis*. . . "

Murugan now took over the conversation, talking long and excitedly, of how the story of Jacob is full of arcane knowledge of Magick and medicine. He reminded me of Joseph's skill in the interpretation of dreams. Even the story of the *Exodus* was really an account of a magical battle in which the Hebrew priests routed their Egyptian colleagues.

"Yes," I said, "I know all this, but has it really anything to do with the holy men of south India?"

Murugan paused. "Well," he said, "its up to you what you believe. I am merely answering your question. That is where the Siddha doctrine, as taught to me by my teacher, originates. In this I have no doubt. If you have doubts then you must go to your books. But you will find that what I am saying is true. Knowledge is like a river, its origins are obscure."

I told Murugan that I did not doubt what he was saying but that it was the Western way to always seek corroboration. He nodded in agreement.

"Go to your books," he said, "and if I were you I would start by reading about the Romanaka - the Romans."

"The Romans?" I replied, unable to suppress the scepticism in my voice.

"Yes," my Guru said, "the Romans. Have you not heard of Sir Mortimer Wheeler?"

I nodded.

"The greatest discovery of his life was the presence of the Romans here in this part of India. You will see."

And indeed I did.

from *Isis In India*

Introduction

'In the Shaivite tradition, the God's companions (Kaulas) are described as a troupe of freakish, adventurous delinquent and wild young people, who prowl in the night, shouting in the storm, singing, dancing and ceaselessly playing outrageous tricks on sages and Gods. They are called Ganas, the 'vagabonds', corresponding to the Cretan Korybantes and the Celtic Korrigans (fairies' sons). Like the Sileni and Satyrs, some of them have goat's or bird's feet. The Ganas mock the rules of ethics and social order. They personify the joy of living, courage and imagination, which are all youthful values. They live in harmony with Nature and oppose the destructive ambition of the city and the deceitful moralism which both hides and expresses it. These delinquents of heaven are always there to restore true values and to assist the 'God-mad' who are persecuted and mocked by the powerful. They personify everything which is feared by and displeases bourgeois society and which is contrary to the good morale of a well-policed city and its palliative concepts.'

From *Shiva and Dionysus* by Shri Alain Daniélou
(reprinted as *Gods of Love and Ecstasy*) page 99

2. What is Tantra?

The term Tantra is traditionally applied to a group of Hindu and Buddhist mystical texts which, along with numerous other topics, deal at length with the spiritual value of carnal knowledge, which taken literally means that gnosis obtained through the whole body. ('Gnosis' is a key magical concept and can be defined as knowledge obtained by direct perception through magick (qv), in other words the magical mind.) Practitioners of Tantra are freethinkers known by various names including Tantriks (magicians), Kaulas (companions of the Gods), Nāthas (Adepts) or Siddhas (powerful ones). Tantriks study and practice Magick and thus they find a great deal of common ground with western magical adepts. Tantra is also a religious inclination and pre-eminent amongst the deities worshipped within Hindu Tantrism are Śiva, Śaktī the primordial Goddess, but also the synthesis, child or prince e.g. the elephant headed deity Gaṇeśa. Genuine followers of Tantra believe that our psychological make-up has male and female components and attempt to realize the full potential of this bisexual nature with their own lives and bodies.

Following the popularity of the ideas of Carl Jung this may not seem such a startling hypothesis, but it should be borne in mind that these ideas are in Asia over a thousand years old. The Tantrik attempts to unify the male and female sides of the mind/body and thus achieve what is acknowledged to be a primal state of innocence/gnosis. Magick and sometimes sexuality are used to bring about this transformation. Tantrik texts almost always begin with a dialogue between Śiva and Śaktī. One can infer from this that the human worshipper, whatever their gender, assumes the god-form of one of these, either Śiva or Śaktī, in order to participate anew in the flow of knowledge from the divine.

As a cult or sect Tantrism is difficult to pin down. Like Hinduism it is really a collection of different practices and philosophical attitudes. To confuse things further some elements of Tantra can be found even amongst more orthodox worshippers. There are eight characteristic practices or techniques found in Tantra: They are: Sādhana, Mantra, Maṇḍala, Mudrā, Nyāsa, Dhyāna, Pūja and Dīkshā. If one understands the meaning of each of these unfamiliar Sanskrit words, one has a fairly good idea of what being a Tantrik entails.

i. Sādhana/practice

Tantra is an individual and above all a practical road to liberation. The primary means of achieving this is by the practice of Kuṇḍalini Yoga of the kind described in *The Serpent Power* (q.v.). Despite its emphasis on the practical as opposed to the theoretical side of spirituality, it would be wrong to suppose that Tantra is simple. For example the discipline of medicine, which is much admired by Tantriks, would take at least seven years of intensive practical study, including the study of large ancient medical textbooks. Medicine, Astrology, Magick and Alchemy are some of the practical attainments much prized within Tantra. What has been termed 'results Magick' (Phala) is particularly important for some Tantriks, the so-called six acts, achieved by devotion to the appropriate Shakti are: Pacification, Subjugation, Immobilization, Spreading Discord, Driving Away, Liquidation. The Vīṇīnashikha Tantra (q.v.) has more details of this aspect of Tantrism and also includes a typical sectarian practice to the God Tumburu, who has been identified with the Śiva cult. Devotees of Tumburu are said to be skilled at dealing with various types of fever (jvara), a disease not uncommon in medieval and indeed modern Asia.

ii. Mantra

Mantra is one of the chief instruments of Tantrism. It should not be confused with 'twilight' language although there is some overlap. Some say the word comes from 'Man' to think and 'Tra' instrument. According to Alain Daniélou, Mantra literally means 'thought-form'. Mantra is an intricate series of sounds which are vibrated or sung in a special manner. Some older authorities thought that Mantras were meaningless and irrational; Bharati rejects this contention. For example the apparently meaningless Mantra 'Hrīm' is always addressed to Shakti and may well come from the Indian root 'Hrī' meaning modesty. Some Mantras are onomatopoeic e.g.'Phat', the Tantrik means of driving away negative energies. Others may be derived from animal sounds as for example three of the seven notes in the Indian musical scale. There is an elaborate theory, based on the analysis of the Sanskrit alphabet to account for their phonic power. In common with many other Eastern religions, Tantra maintains that sound has a magical quality and is one of the fundamental creative principles of the cosmos. Furthermore, it is widely held in Hinduism that the Gods do not like to be addressed directly by name or as the ancient sage Yājñavalkya said 'the Gods are fond of obscurity.' Closely related to this is the idea that any divine thing can be reduced to an essential seed or essence. This is analogous to the methods of the pharmacist who attempts to isolate the active principle in any compound. The active principle in a Mantra 'compound' is called a seed or Bīja. For example the seed Mantra for the elephant-headed God Gaṇeśa is Gaṇ. A seed Mantra can be created by taking the first letter of a deity's name and adding nasal 'm' e.g. Dum for Durga etc. Further reading see Mircea Eliade's *Yoga, Immortality and Freedom.*

iii. Maṇḍala or Yantra

Typical of Tantrism and indeed of other magical traditions, is the extended use of intricate geometric designs of various sizes. Such diagrams are sometimes able to generate their own kind of *gnosis.* Many examples are reproduced in books although in reality they come in two or three dimensional representations of a deity or cosmos. A Maṇḍala should be laid flat on the floor for magical use and not hung up behind an altar. Maṇḍala means diagram, a Yantra is a tool or device, and would therefore include things like Maṇḍalas and a whole lot more besides.

iv. Mudrā

The use of mystical hand gestures and postures such as those found in Yoga, it would take a whole book to describe them all. The 'Horned God' Mudrā of Wicca is in fact one of the very oldest. Pointing fingers, raised hands and intricate interlocking of the fingers as in the yoni mudrā all play their part. This also raises the subject of the Tantrik predilection for euphemisms or so-called 'twilight language'. Mudrā is also a name for one of the five strong enjoyments found in Tantrik worship and may be a euphemism for sacred sexuality as opposed to reproductive sex. The breaking of taboos is another characteristic of Tantrism.

v. Nyāsa

This is a very distinctive part of Tantrism and one that is often overlooked. Nyāsa means *placing* and takes many forms for example the 'installation' of the sacred power of a deity into a mystical drawing or maṇḍala. This same energy can also be placed by one participant in a ritual into the body of another. There are also elaborate and sometimes secret methods of touching parts of the body whilst intoning the appropriate mantra. This is a kind of purification rite. A solitary practitioner uses many such techniques and vivifies his or her maṇḍala by 'taking' the personal God energy (iśṭadevatā) from the region of their heart and placing it on the altar. Here we can detect the practical counterpart of the mystical doctrine of microcosm and macrocosm. The body is viewed as a miniature version of the cosmos, and thus by installing the appropriate deities and elements, the body becomes a *living* maṇḍala.

vi. Dhyāna

This can be translated as meditation but Tantrik meditation soon passes beyond the more austere variety set forth in for example Patañjali's *Yoga Sūtras* and later versions of it in Vivekananda and even Aleister Crowley. Tantrik meditation uses rather than suppresses the senses. Dhyāna also means the image of the God or Goddess as handed down from previous practitioners. Closely related to this is the typical Tantrik practice of internal pilgrimage, the constructing of an internal mental or astral temple, peopled by the Gods and in which worship and Magick occurs. In some instances whole landscapes are created and the Tantrik with sufficient mental stamina is able to undertake an extended pilgrimage through the sacred and *erotic landscape*

vii. Pūja

Tantriks are magicians and experience shows that Magick needs the practice of physical rituals to ground it and to really make it work. Pūja could be a communal ritual with other Tantriks in which, traditionally, special regard was given to the Shaktis or Yogini, female participant, human and 'demonic'. For example the five 'Makāras' literally 'Ms' - in Sanskrit, the first letter of a word denoting powerful enjoyments such as meat, fish, wine, sexual intercourse, non-reproduction, public breaking of taboos.

viii. Dīkshā

This means initiation and in the past great importance was placed on the need for proper initiation by a qualified Guru, i.e. one who is part of a recognized tradition (Sampradāya) and has the right to confer the desired initiation (Parampayā). Initiation might also place an obligation to be part of a particular cult, deity or group guardian.

Magick and Liberation

What is called Tantra in the East has a great deal in common with the Hermetic magical tradition of the West. There are many definitions of Magick. One of the most widely respected comes from Aleister Crowley. Crowley wrote that 'Magick was the science and art of causing change in conformity with will.' Magick is a set of techniques, some of them very ancient, that help us humans change our consciousness at will. It is an axiom of magical belief that human consciousness and reality are mysteriously linked. By changing consciousness it is also possible to change the world in which we live.

There are two basic kinds of Magick, both of which are found within Tantrism. The first, most common aim or use of Magick is called results Magick. For example a Witch's spell is often a piece of results Magick. The real core of Magick is an individual spiritual quest for immortality and liberation (Moksha). Ritual is one of the most important techniques of magical practice. Through ritual the Magician learns to decondition his or her Self, stripping away outmoded beliefs in order to be aligned with real cosmic forces. Following on from this is 'Svecchācara', an important tenet of Kaulas and Nāthas:

Svecchācara

An important concept of the Nātha cult goes by the Sanskrit word Svecchācara – 'the path of one's own will'. The use of this concept is very ancient within our tradition. I think it is legitimate to compare it to the idea of 'Thelema' or the 'True Will' within the modern revived cult of Magick set in motion in modern times by Aleister Crowley.

Tantrik traditions and sects

There are many groups and individuals who claim to teach or practice Tantrik methods of liberation. AMOOKOS, the Arcane and Magical Order of the Knights of Shamballa is an East-West Kaula group with a genuine line of initiation leading back to Matsyendranātha, who lived sometime between the years 700 to 900 of our era.

Tantrism has gone through a number of 'reforms' since the creation of the practice in the first few centuries of the common era. For our own tradition the evolution is from Kula (clan) to Kaula Scholars such as Alexis Sanderson have 'argued that the Kaula current is in fact a domesticated version of a more radical cremation-ground culture, and the adoption of the Kāpālika-Bhairava—with all his gruesome imagery —

as its highest metaphysical principle is perhaps the most telling indication of this. What is striking nevertheless is the scrupulous retention of this symbolic universe through visualization, substitutions, semantic equations, and so on. In their radical versions, these sex rites were practiced in the cremation-grounds and could even make use of corpses. In Abhinava's description, however, the whole imagery is internalized, through a play on the word *citi* which means both funeral pyre and (the supreme) consciousness (Sunthar Visuvallingam: 2003).

The Kaulas developed into 4 main systems:

1. Kaula Trika

The Kaula system centers around the cult of Bhairava, the ferocious form of the God Shiva. If one had to characterize the Kaula point of view it would be that reality is viewed from the vantage point of the root chakra. Thus instead of internalized solar and lunar channels, a Kaula could use external female and male 'secret' substances to go beyond time and place. Technically the Kaula system is involved not only in the ascent of Kuṇḍalini—but also its descent back into the external world—then one sees everything as the play of Śiva.

For the Kaula the adjunct 'eat meat and drink wine' means to ground amrita via actual external rituals while at the same time internalizing it then exteriorizing it via descent of the amrita.

2. Kālī cult of Mata, Krama and Guhyakālī

The Krama is an expanded version of Sāṁkhya—the Hindu 'Tree of Life'. One learns to see infinity in all objects and slowly regains the Godhead by means of ascent through the 36 'Tattvas' or 'levels of existence'. It is a more gradual path (as opposed to a 'sudden' path). Each mentation associated with any object has 12 'Kalis' or movements of the mind. The Krama was first introduced at the beginning of the Kali Yuga, but then was lost. It was reintroduced by Śivanāndanātha in the 7th century AD.

3. Kubjikā

This path is largely lost and was the cult of the 'Hunched back one'.

4. Tripurāsundarī

The cult of Tripurāsundarī is the cult of Lalitā as associated with the Śrī Cakra or Śrī Yantra. Its current popular version is largely connected to Brahmanism and has been stripped of many of its more exotic Kaula elements (meat, wine, etc.). It has in particular become affiliated and institutionalized by the Shankarācharya seat of the South (Vajranātha: 2003).

Recommended Reading

(Mainly books with some connection to the AMOOKOS tradition, either by way of content or the affiliation of the author.)

AMOOKOS' *Tantra Magick* (out of print, but can be read in some libraries.)

Arthur Avalon, *The Serpent Power – The Secrets of Tantric and Shaktic Yoga* (Dover)
Basham, A. L., *The Wonder that was India* (Sidgwick and Jackson).
Callasso, Roberto, *Ka* (Vintage) not a bad intro to the ocean of Indian mythology.
Dadaji (c1989)*The Amoral Way of Wizardry,* (Sweden).
Daniélou, Alain (1991)*Gods & Myths of India - Hindu Polytheism,* (Inner Traditions, Vermont).
Daniélou, Alain, *Shiva and Dionysus* (Inner Traditions, Vermont).
Georg Feuerstein (1990) *Yoga, techniques of Ecstasy,* East West.
Fries, Jan (1996) *Seidways, shaking, swaying and serpent mysteries* (Mandrake of Oxford).
Fries, Jan (1992) *Visual Magick* (Mandrake of Oxford) - although they are not written from the Tantrik point of view, contains many useful techniques of Magick.
Briggs, G. W. (1938, 1989) *Gorakhnāth & the Kamphata Yogīs,* Varanasi.
Magee (trans) & P. C. Bagchi, *Kaulajñana-nirṇaya of the school of Matsyendranātha* (Tantra Granthamala No 12).
Magee (trans) *Vāmakeshvarīmatam* (*Tantra Granthamala* No 11).
Magee, Mike, *Tantrik Astrology* (Mandrake of Oxford).
Patañjali, *The Yoga Sūtras.*
Shual, Katon, *Sexual Magick* (Mandrake of Oxford).
Tawney C. H., (trans) *Vikram & Vetala* – 'King Vikram and the Ghost'.
White, David Gordon (1996) *The Alchemical Body: Siddha Traditions in Medeival India* (University of Chicago Press).
Svoboda, Robert E. (1986) *Aghora - at the left hand of God,* (Brotherhood of Life).

2. Sādhana

The heart of Tantra is Sādhana. Effective Sādhana cannot be accomplished without an initiation (Dīkshā) from a qualified Guru. This book is designed to act as a taster and to provide a short body of work suitable for the period of about one month. The lunar calendar is especially important within Tantrism and you should aim to begin your practice on an appropriate lunar day (see my *Tankhem* trilogy for more on lunar Mysteries). I'm assuming that you already have some kind of magical journal or diary in which you make notes and record your experiences. I also recommend that you use something like the lunar sheets reproduced in the appendix on the lunar calendar). This encourages you to observe the phases of the moon on any particular solar day. This is a simplified version of the Kalās and is not, strictly speaking, the same as the lunar Kalās which require quite a complex lunar observation (tithis) from an ephemeris.

The East-West Tantrik Order AMOOKOS developed a rite of self-initiation that could be done at an appropriate time and coordinated with an experienced mentor within the Order. I'm going to suggest that you use a modified form of that rite for a *temporary* dedication as a mitra or friend of the Nathās. If you do have a name you intend to use for magical experimentations you might like to append the suffix -mitra to that name for the purposes of this present work.

A Tantrik ritual, like any, begins with an opening rite. The obscure and difficult to come by book *Tantra Magick* has such a ritual. Bur for convenience I will give an example of my own opening rite, which is, in part, derived from *Tantra Magick*. Spend some time reading through the rubrik and make preparations to start on an appropriate phase (Kalā) of the moon. I intend to add various elements to the Sādhana throughout the book, so that by the end of the month you will have accomplished a fairly complicated Tantrik practice.

The opening rite

Preparing the temple. A quiet room or space with a simple altar. Some lamps or candles, incense, water and flowers. If you would like an image of the divine and at this stage are not sure what to use, then I suggest a stylized pair of oriental wooden sandals or footprints, that can be painted an appropriate colour, in this case start with red.

It's always a good idea to do some sort of physical warmup before starting any kind of meditation or ritual. I would recommend some simple yoga exercises beginning with just standing up completely straight like a tree (vṛiksānana) making sure you stretch upwards through the very top of your head, the chin being kept tucked in. You can if you like imagine that some power grasps a tuft of hair on the very crown of your head and gently lifts and elongates your spine. Perhaps this becomes a meditation in its own right, as you imagine the vegetative power of the tree, drawing nutrients from the earth via its roots and both releasing and absorbing oxygen and cosmic energy via its leaves. After this I recommend you spend a few minutes gently warming the main muscles groups, especially the neck and shoulders, the hips, groin, knees etc. Tensing and relaxing, gently rotating, that kind of thing.

Follow this with a more formal exercise sequence usually called the *Sun Salutation* (Sūryana Maskar). If you have access to a yoga teacher you should be able to get some pointers on this very useful technique. Basically it involves stretching upwards to greet the sun, then 'following' the breath as you move forward into a loose forward bend, flexing your knees, your hands find the earth in front of you. Now supporting your weight with your hands, slide or wiggle your feet back so you are in a relaxed prostrate position, laying face down on the floor, from this, and 'following the breath' you come back to the forward bend position and then come up slowly, unfolding the spine, one vertebrae at a time, continue the stretch upwards, reaching up and finally bringing the hands down to your chest in the gesture of prayer known in the Hindu tradition as 'Añjali' . That cycle represents one salutation (to the Sun). Do this an appropriate number of times, depending on your fitness and intention. Your body should feel energised and may have a slight tremor, especially in the thighs. This trembling sensation is very useful to the Magician, we could almost call it 'shamanic trembling' as it is a phenomenon attested in many diverse magical traditions.

Now think for a moment of the power of the North and the constellation of the Saptaṛiṣi, the seven sages or *Ursa Major* in modern parlance. Perhaps reach up to the north and draw down some of its power. Then face East say:

> 'I honor the line of innumerable Nāthas and cast a circle of dragon's glow, may this circle be intact and the peace of Śiva/Śaktī dwell herein.'

Vibrate the Mantra

oṁ
three times. followed by
namo Śivāya,
namo Śaktīya,

namo namas

oṁ, oṁ, oṁ

Vibrating of a Mantra is a basic magical skill. The best way to grasp what is required is to actually hear another more experienced magician vibrating. You can get lots of hints on the practice from books such as Aleister Crowley's *Liber ABA/Magick*, appendix entitled *Liber O;* the works of Israel Regardie. Or listen to the liturgy of Eastern Orthodox religions, especially Judaism, for hints on the technique.

Sound has a very special role with Tantrism and Hinduism. The ancient Magi believed that everything was ultimately composed of sound and that sound therefore has a particularly magical quality. Perhaps you have heard the Buddhist puzzle 'what is the sound of one hand clapping?' - well if I tell you that in Tantrism there are said to be two kinds of sound - the struck and the unstruck - perhaps you can work out the answer to the riddle?

Exercise 1: Yoga of the voice

Whatever, I suggest you break off now and practice your vibration. Vibrate the Mantra oṁ over and over. Try it in the bath or when you are out alone in the woods. Written down in the Roman script it looks quite terse, but the Sanskrit phoneme is actually a lot more complex. The Mantra oṁ should involve pretty much every element or articulation of the voice. Here is the Mantra in the original script - even if you

ओं

know nothing of Sanskrit perhaps you can sense its composite nature?
It starts as a low vibration in the lowest ranges of the abdomen and flows upwards through the chest, throat, etc and hums away in the upper nasal bones where it sets off lots of strange tones and overtones.
Try it now, elongate the phonemes something like
oooooooooooooooo
mmmmmmmmmm
nnnnnnnn
gggggggggggg
hhhhhhhhh
If you are not used to singing, you will find your voice is not yet very smooth. But the vocal chords are muscles and can be strengthed through appropriate use. Ie the more you practice the better your voice will become - and the more magically effective your vibration of mantra will be. Appropriate posture will also play a crucial role in the power and dynamism of the voice. For further reading on the Yoga of the voice see *The Voice Book*, by Michael McCallion (Faber).

Quarter Guardians

The vibration of Mantras and the God names above will have created a rich matrix of sound on which to lay the next part of our rite. It is now time to summon or visualize four guardians of the directions. In the Tantrik tradition, any particular Sādhana or practice will have its own appropriate guardians of the directions. All Tantrik rituals must begin with an invocation to the Primal Gatekeeper, the elephant headed God Gaṇeśa. So even a rite directed to the Goddess Kālī, needs a preliminary invocation to Gaṇeśa. Luckily the oṁ Mantra we have just learnt is also a manifestation of Gaṇeśa. And as this Mantra is extremely common and invariably occurs as the first word in many longer Mantras, for example the famous *oṁ mane padme oṁ*, we can be sure that this ritual requirement is already achieved.

The quarter guardians of Tantrism are almost always auspicious couples, shown either in loving (mithuna) or sexual (maithuna) embrace. If you look at Indian architecture you should be able to recognise this feature amongst the *apparent* chaos of symbols.

In the Nātha tradition the basic ritual zone is protected by the following entities:

> In the East she is golden and 'rides' the human form of the God Śiva,
> In the South she is red and rides a lion
> In the West she rides a blue eagle
> In the North a green bull

Take some time now to write out a sentence or two with which to summon and welcome these four auspicious couples to witness your rite and guard your circle. It will be something like:

> I honour the beautiful Goddess of the East, the Śaktī of Air. I see you adorned with all adornments, naked, her beautiful skin smeared with yellow paste, and in sexual union with the Man-God Śiva.

Continue and write a similar phrase for each of the quarters. When you're ready, stand making the gesture known as 'Añjali', basically hands palms together in the gesture of prayer over the heart Chakra. You will need to form an image in your mind of the four guardians as you say the words you have composed. In the Kaula/Nātha tradition there are no images available of these entities as it is thought better that each practitioners constructs or reveals his own form of the guardians.

Visualisation

Magick requires a good imagination. Another of its basic skills is the ability to visualise. Of the eight 'signs' of the Tantrik described earlier (see if you can remember them without looking) visualisation is encompassed by Dhyāna. As was said with vibration, we could almost say that visualisation relies upon an internal organ that becomes stronger the more it is exercised. Many Magicians have trouble with visualisation, in part because of poor descriptions of the technique in older books on Magick. I put it to you that you would not abandon speaking because your voice was poor. You might rather persevere until your voice improved. I suggest the same attitude is appropriate when approaching visualisation.

It is common across many magical traditions to combine sounds with certain gestures. It's a good idea to do this kind of thing when opening the quarters. As Katon Shual reminds us in his *Sexual Magick*, bodily techniques are the necessary conditions for certain mystical inner states. The basic oṁ Mantra used above has its own Mudrā or physical gesture - something like a simple praying gesture Añjali. There are several other sets of opening gestures that are useful in this context. Tantrik workship involves a great many obscure body 'Mudrās'. The following sequence is borrowed from the *Greek Magical Papyri*, and comprises a series of signs to accompany the seven basic vowel sounds. It might seem an odd insertion but both traditions used the basic vowel chanting that was once part of an international language of Magick. Sometimes I augment this with some body gestures, vibrating vowels for each of the cardinal points and above below and in the heavens. This ritual called the Rite of the Heptagram was known in Ancient Egypt.

Face North and think of the constellation *Ursa Major*, which represents the seven primary ṛiṣis or sages of the Ancient Hindu and Egyptian traditions. To remember the seven vowels I recommend the following mnemonic:

FAther GEt GAme to FEEd the HOt NEw hOme.

1. Now turn to the East, form both hands into fists and raise them up and to the left of your head, now vibrate the first vowel long and hard - AAAAAAA.

2. Now turn to the North and stretching your right hand in front of you vibrate the second vowel EEEEEEE, using the mnemoic gEt as above.

3. Then turn to the West and extend both hands in front of you and vibrate ÊÊÊÊÊÊÊas in GAme.

4. Then turn to the South and drawing both hands to your stomach vibrate IIIIII as in fEEd.

[Whether one remains facing South or returns to face the East depends upon the operation in hand].

5. Now bend over and reach out to the Earth vibrating OOOOOOO as in HOt.

6. Then gradually unfolding, come up and place your hands on your heart and vibrate YYYYYYY as in NEw.

7. Finally stretching up to the heavens vibrate Ô Ô Ô Ô Ô Ô Ô as in HÔme.

(Now make the sign of the (invoking) pentagram in the air in front of you and vibrate
Ou, Eye, EE, Aa, Uh)

Turn to the North, bow and visualise the form of a naked young Goddess with a peaceful smiling face, her skin is green and she sits on the back of a bull.

(Again make the sign of the (invoking) pentagram and vibrate: Ou, Eye, EE, Aa, Uh).

Turn to the East, bow and visualise the form of a naked young Goddess with a peaceful smiling face, her skin is golden as she sits astride the God Shiva.

(Again make the sign of the (invoking) pentagram and vibrate: Ou, Eye, EE, Aa, Uh).

Turn to the South, bow and visualise the form of naked young goddess with skin the colour of fire. With flaming eyes, who sits astride a lion.

(Again make the sign of the (invoking) pentagram and vibrate: Ou, Eye, EE, Aa, Uh).

Turn to the West, bow and visualise the form of a naked young Goddess, blue in colour, glistening with moisture, with large beautiful eyes, riding a goose or swan.

(Again make the sign of the (invoking) pentagram and vibrate: Ou, Eye, EE, Aa, Uh).

Finally

Honour the Earth, bending over, touching the Earth say 'O' as in 'rope'
and then the Sky, having both hands on your head say 'Ô' as in 'bow'.

The Astral Temple

It may well take you a while to get all of the above techniques working well for you. But when you do you should find that you can open your circle in a few minutes of intense activity. It is probably best to have some work to do within the sacred space. Another useful magical task is to begin the process of developing an astral temple appropriate to the work in hand. You may already be using some such temple and there is a discussion of the technique in my book *Sexual Magick*. For the puposes of the short programme of work I suggest using the basic Tantrik astral temple below:

The Kāmarūpa Temple Meditation

Preamble

Here is a concept in Magick whose importance cannot be overemphasised - the construction of a imaginary counterpart to your physical temple.[1]

Every style of Magick has its own particular astral temple. In Kabbalah I have heard it called the Malkuth temple, and its description is based upon the mystical drawing called the Tree of Life. In Chaos Magick it is the Chaos Sphere; in Greek

Magick it could be the *Tetraktys*. In Thelema the astral temple could well be based on the description given in *Liber Al* I.51. The Renaissance magus Giordano Bruno coined the term 'Theatre of Memory' for this concept. He designed, in his mind's eye, an imaginary Greek theatre, where every part had symbolic significance. He could use this technique to memorise the relationship between very complex groups of symbols. Similar images were used by John Dee and Robert Fludd, see for instance Palladio's reconstruction of the theatre of Vitruvious or even the plans of Shakespeare's Globe theatre.[2] This is a very important discovery.

The basic design of the Tantrik astral temple is the Śrī Yantra, the most famous and universal of all the mystical diagrams (Maṇḍala or Yantra). If you are not familiar with this diagram, then it is reproduced above. I am indebted to blessed Gaṇeśa, the elephant-headed One, for revealing to me some of its significance.

Becoming familiar with the lineaments of the astral temple, is usually accomplished by the repeated practice of guided visualisation or so-called 'pathworking'. This is where the experimenter (sādhaka) imagines him or herself walking or moving through the designated landscape or building in serial order. Thus at first only the lower parts of the glyph are traversed, building up a great familiarity with its topography. As one grows in mental stamina and ability, higher and higher levels of the glyph are opened up to the explorer.

It is possible to obtain pre-recorded tapes of famous pathworkings, which are designed so that the experimenter (sādhaka) may follow the imagery as it unfolds. In my experience this kind of pre-recorded guided visualisation is of limited use. The more the experimenter (sādhaka) gets into the pathworking, the more distracting becomes the voice on the tape. The speaker may insist that the statue has an angry face, when you've already seen it, and it is smiling! The answer is perhaps to read (or play) the description once or twice, and then do the pathworking without the tape. Alternatively the guide can lead you to a particular door, describing what is behind the door and then invite you to step through it alone, and explore it at your own pace. The guide then remains silent. The best examples of this are done in rituals, and the guide has been chosen beforehand and will often not read from a prearranged script but will improvise with what comes into their head, a kind of stream of consciousness. When the guide stops talking, the group can lapse into their own meditation or pathworking. So what the guide is saying is not scripted, it is what they are 'seeing' or intuiting - they are in fact in a low level trance, which can often deepen significantly when they lapse into silence.

When the guide invites you to proceed on your own, do so. Follow the vision, however feeble, to its natural conclusion. The session usually terminates when you reach your goal or begin to run out of mental stamina and feel the need to wind things up. During this time, you may have become quite dissassociated from your physical body. Perhaps it is some physical sensation, such as pins and needles that disturbs you, or the subtle movements of others in the room who have obviously finished. Alternatively, you may hear a gentle sounding of a bell chimed by one of the other participants, as the pre-arranged signal to return. When either of these things happens, try and mentally retrace your steps to where the guided visualisation began.

When you have done this, become fully aware of your body again and if necessary vibrate or chant some sacred words to really ground yourself. It is especially important to join in with any chanting at the end of the ritual where appropriate, or do your closing, as this serves to balance everything up again and prevent unwanted obsession.

Transition

You need to develop an image that represents the transition from your normal mindscape to that of the astral temple. To do this you must accept the following fantasy - your temple room or bedroom is an individual hut or tent in a wooded clearing. When you have done your opening rite, settle down and close your eyes. 'Look' around your room in your mind's eye and see the changes. The walls of your hut are strangely familiar. You see the door by which you came in, but also a curtain hand-woven from three fabrics, one is browny red, the other is white and the third is black. Imagine yourself approaching this curtain, but before touching, trace the symbol of earth[3] upon it and then draw it aside. Behind this is an old wooden door, with a bolt. Unbolt the door and pass through.

Look around. You are in a very large enclosure. It is the outer enclosure wall or temenos of a temple. The high walls are of ancient crenelated stone.

How large is the space? It can be quite compact or as extensive as the footprint of the great pyramids of Ancient Egypt. Beyond you can see a wall of mountains that surrounds on all sides the valley in which this temple is built. Beyond the mountains you see sky and clouds. This is an incredibly safe place for you. Whenever you have need of sanctuary on an inner level, this is the image to call to mind. Take some time to wander around the enclosure, taking note of some of these details, and recording them in your magical diary.

Make a mental note of the time of day; the season of the year; the weather. Are there any other people present? Do any supernatural beings appear, if so what happens? When you first 'see' your astral temple, where are you, i.e. East, West, North, South, whatever?

[By the way, if you feel you've 'seen' enough and really need to stop, simply go back to the door and curtain (your deep mind will know where it is) visualise it one last time, pass through it back into your meditation room. Sit down. Visualise the seal of earth glowing on the curtain cloth then fading and come back to yourself, as before. Vibrate oṁ three times to really ground yourself.]

If you are ready to see the rest of the temple, this is some of what can been seen:

If you explore you will find a square communal bathing place, with seven steps leading down to the murky water. But before you can go there, you must pay the Bath Keeper.

Look at the Bath Keeper. With a nod of recognition you see the elephant headed God, Gaṇeśa. You push a coin into his hand, and he invites you to continue. You walk slowly down the seven steps, removing your clothing as you go. There in the water you can see frogs, fish and other swimming creatures. You see a shoal of fish moving together, then breaking the surface of the water with their heads, looking for a moment, then dashing off under the surface. You wash away your memories in the water of forgetfulness, wash away the worry and problems of the mundane world. Do all these things in your imagination.

When you finish, step out of the waist-deep water on the other side where someone hands you some clean clothes. Climb out of the bath and continue to explore until you find a group of sixty-four small shrines arranged around a central space. Each shrine is more or less identical. Each is equi-distant from a slightly raised central platform that is open to the sky. The doorway of each is shielded by a curtain and faces the central circle. You are drawn to the centre of the shrine complex, to the circular plinth.

As you approach you can see evidence of devotion. You can also see the lines of the Śrī Yantra. You have a moment alone, and can leave an offering if you have one, perhaps the things you have achieved today. This offering could also be in the form of a flower or petal. Before leaving it you must breathe some of your spirit into it using the Tantrik Nyāsa technique[5].

Your devotion finished, you circumambulate the shrine. Look around you, across the temple, to the landscape beyond. Now if you wish, you may return again to whence you came back to your meditation room and waiting body. As you return you are given a small edible gift (prasāda) which you may eat immediately or keep for later.

Every day of your practice you should aim to return to the temple, make your oblation, receive your gift from the temple and return. Each time note whether anything has changed. Does anyone say anything to you, do strange things happen, how do you feel? Note it all down in your diary.

To finish absorb all entities and guardians into yourself and say:

'I close this umbra zonule.
May all experience
peace, freedom and happiness
in the name of Śiva/Śaktī.'

Then vibrate oṁ three times.

Do not expect the image to be very sharp at this stage. Even if your powers of visualisation are initially very feeble they will develop if you give them a chance. Even if it seems that you are 'making' it happen, and that most of your mind is still very much rooted in the real world, try to go with it, like a favourite daydream.

The Kalās

In the 1970s, Kenneth Grant wrote a book about Crowley that did much to awaken interest in the Tantrik current within Thelemic Magick. The book was called *Aleister Crowley and the Hidden God* and it contains an account of the system called the Kalās, thought by many to be an extension of the Tantrik Kuṇḍalini Yoga. Kalās means part or aspect, and is used in Tantrik literature to refer to the subsidiary aspects of the Primal Goddess, for example those corresponding to the eight petals on the Śrī Yantra, or in an example given by Bharati, ten aspects arranged on the intersecting triangles of the Yantra.[6] Another important meaning of Kalā is in Kalyāṇamalla *Anaṅgaraṅga - Arena of the Love God.* This book was written in the sixteenth century as a updated version of the *Kāmasūtra* written sometime between the second century BCE and the second century CE. Whilst the *Kāmasūtra* contains many important sexual Magick themes, including body piercing and body striking, it is on the whole a manual of courtly love. It was clearly written before Tantrism was created or rediscovered (whichever theory you prefer). The *Anaṅgaraṅga*, on the other hand was written after Tantrism had reached its zenith and therefore contains many Tantrik ideas. Like many ancient erotic texts they are written by men observing women and they can seem cold and clinical. It is hard to imagine real sexual beings consulting the calendar before they make love in order to work out which part of their lover's body they should caress. These reservations aside, we can say that the core of erotic texts like the *Anaṅgaraṅga* stem from the observations all lovers naturally make of the ebb and flow of desire and the variations through the day, month and year in the way one experiences a lover's body. This may include changes in taste, feel, smell etc. Anyway, for what it's worth here is the section in the *Anaṅgaraṅga* that details some of these variations. I would suggest that a matrix could also be drawn up for a man's body, I would welcome the reader's own observations on this.

> 1. Speaking generally from the full moon day the Candrakalā[7] descends by the left side of the woman from the forehead through the eyes, cheeks, lips, chin, neck, shoulder, arm-pit, breast, the side, hip, pubic region, genitals, knee, ankle and foot; on the new moon day it starts the upward course by the right side in a like manner and reaches the forehead on the full moon day.
>
> 2-3. When the position of the Candrakalā in a woman is in her scalp, her passion should be roused by gently touching the hair like a comb; if it is in the eyes, cheeks and lips then these should be kissed passionately; if it is in her neck or arm-pit, it should be marked with your fingernail. If in the breast, waist, side and hip these should be pressed with firm hands. The navel should be petted with your palm, if in the genitals the tongue should be pressed inside the vagina and it should be sucked. If in the chest it should be gently struck, pubic

region with your own pubis, thumb with your thumb, feet should be pressed with your feet. By arousing the erogenous zones a man who is well versed in the art of love will capture a woman's heart and both will derive maximum pleasure.' In these ideas from *Anaṅgaraṅga* there is perhaps an echo of the Kāmarūpa temple.

Notes

1 The Islamic scholar Henry Corbin has written a very interesting essay on the power of the myth of the lost or destroyed temple. He begins with a quote from the Talmud, which says that when the Romans destroyed the second temple, it was a disaster not merely for the Jews but for the whole human race. Actually the real disaster may have occurred when Nebuchadnezzar burnt the first Solomonic temple and the priests returned the keys to the angelic beings, thus breaking one of the last direct links between Gods and humanity. This is a recurrent myth, one in which the earth no longer contains the divine temple but has become its crypt. This myth contains within it the entire aim of Magick. See Henry Corbin, 'L'Imago Templi', *Spring* Vol 43 (1974); 'La Configuration du Temple de la Ka'ba comme secret de la vie spirituelle' Spring, Vol 34 (1965). Both these articles are in English and are reprinted in the *Eranos-Jahrbuch.*

2 See Frances Yates, *The Art of Memory.*

3 Choose this for yourself, I use an equal armed cross in a circle.

4 Nyāsa - placing. In simplest form, visualise your self-chosen deity appearing in the region of your heart. When this is clear, imagine that it begins to move in time with your in and out breath. With each breath it moves a little further, until you breathe it out through your left nostril and 'catch' it on a prepared flower petal and can then gently guide it to the image. At the end of the ritual, reverse this process.

5 Bharati, A (1970) p. 254

6 Means literally moon-period or time although usually translated as erogenous zone. The allusion is to the daily waxing or waning of the moon. Sexual desire is likened to a moon, centred in the head, that over the course of a month waxes bigger, moving down through the body until it reaches its peak at the vagina. As the moon wanes, so too does the Kalā, retreating upward through the body.

The Gaṇeśa Practice (Sādhana)

If you accept my theory about the different kinds of Kalās then you will find that the energy of a particular God is always manifested via a particular day of the month. To complete this taster of Tantrik Magick I want now to introduce you to one of the most accessible of Hindu Tantrik deities, and to encourage you to celebrate his day and savour his Kalā as the final part of the practice.

I suggest you use the ritual elements practiced so far, but add the following sectarian things. So make the altar, practice the Mantra, settle down for the visualization, and once in the astral temple pay particular attention to the worship of Gaṇeśa.

The Tantrik ritual calender is lunar in nature. Gaṇeśa's special day is called Gaṇeśa chatur or chaturtha, Gaṇeśa fourth. Four is an inauspicious number, but as far as Gaṇeśa is concerned that doesn't matter, because he is a Tantrik deity and things are not what they seem. Gaṇeśa's chatur is calculated as the fourth day of the moon's bright fortnight, or period from new moon. Gaṇeśa's fourth can be celebrated on this day each month with lunar month Bhādrapada (August/September) as the most special of all the ' fourths' in the year. Appropriate dates are available on request or may be sought via the internet.

It is normal to celebrate this festival for five, seven, ten or twenty one days. In the tradition of the right hand path the first day is the most important. In our LHP tradition the final day is most important. You may if you wish, do something for the days leading up to Gaṇeśa feast day. At the very least establish a special altar with the appropriate things - lights and mirrors and the most common of flowers. Eight is a sacred number to Gaṇeśa. His mythical life story tells us that he has links with eight 'demonic'[1] elephant guardians. The eight male elephants could be visualised as direction guardians, with Shiva and Parvati guarding the upper and lower realms. Their names are:

Kāmāsura (love);
Krodāsura (anger);
Lobhāsura (greed);
Mohāsura (delusion);
Matāsura (intoxication);
Mamāsura (ego);[2]
Abhimāsura (attachment to life).
īśṭāsura (self-chosen demon). [3]

Seed mantra is Gaṇ
oṁ Gaṇeśāya namaḥ

Gaṇeśa Rūpa

You may like to install a special consecrated image (Rūpa) of Gaṇeśa, made of worthless plaster.[4] This is traditional, and in Maharashtra state, which is the main centre of the Gaṇeśa cult in India, craftsmen produce hundreds of thousands of these images every year. The image should be painted with care so that it becomes an object of real value. This talisman should be destroyed at the end of the working which should be on Gaṇeśa's fourth (chatur). In India, this is commonly done by submerging the image in the sea or a local river. Letting go of the images into the unconscious should be the last act of the months sādhana and marks a clear point of transition to the next part.

Here is a suggested visualisation (Dhyāna) of Gaṇeśa which you may incorporate in a daily ritual or meditation:

Imagine an island made of nine precious stones
illumined by the distant light of the setting moon
warmed by the early light of the rising sun [5]
cooled by the four fragrant winds of heaven

A perfumed garden of sandalwood sweetness
enmeshed in fine, leafy creepers and lapped
by the honey-sweet water of paradise.
In the distance vibrates the soft echo of eternal drums.

There, beneath one of those fine, immortal trees
is the primordial lotus, and within is Gaṇeśa
great-bellied, with one tusk and ten arms,
tawny and resplendent, seated within a triangle
within a hexagram, his footstool the lion-faced one.

It may help you to familiarise yourself with Gaṇeśa if you read the following doxology, which was composed by Shantidevi and Katon Shual during a previous puja:[6]

Eight fold Doxology of Gaṇeśa

1. With Modaka,[13] garlands and incense I worship Gaṇeśa , the beloved God with the fawn coloured eyes.

2. With a staff, a lamp and a key, I worship Gaṇeśa , Gatekeeper who removes hindrances.[14]

3. With oil, herbs and water, I worship Gaṇeśa the moon crested Keeper of the Sacred Bath.[15]

4. With wine,Maithuna[16] and lotus flowers, I worship Gaṇeśa monstrous Guardian of Kuṇḍalini.[17]

5. With meat, fish[18] and music, I worship Gaṇeśa, the trickster with the twisted trunk.

6. With sweets, healing herbs and Haldi,[19] I worship Gaṇeśa pot bellied Reliever of Childbirth.

7. With poetry, blood and amulets I worship Gaṇeśa whose single tusk is like a sword.

8. With parched grain,[20] stone and poppies I worship Gaṇeśa with the elephant's mouth, as Lord of the Harvest.[21]

Guardians

In some sects, Gaṇeśa has his own quarter guardian who could be either substituted for the Nātha variety described to you above or used as supplementary guardians much as in the Hermetic Order of the Golden Dawn, the Hexagram ritual followed the Lesser Ritual of the Pentagram. In one tradition Gaṇeśa's guardians are given as:

North = Mahī-Viṣnu
East = Rāma-Sītā
South = Śiva-Pārvatī
West = Rāti-Bhaga

Thus:
Hail Rāma and Sītā in the East
The beautiful Sītā was once abducted by demons
Until the hero Rāma chased them to the eastern border
Then incited by the Gods who guard the directions
You hurl the demons ten heads to the skies

Hail Śiva and Pārvatī in the South,
Pārvatī is a match for the God in all austerities
She rouses Lord Śiva from his yogic trance
He would walk through burning coals to be with her, excited by her presence
His third eye opens and all illusion is destroyed

Hail Rāti and his Goddess in the West
The God of love is attracted by
Her presence
From the union of lovers flows an elixir of immortality

Hail Mahī and Viṣnu in the North
The Goddess who was once lost in the chaotic waters
Until he lifted her up on his giant boar's tusk
There she clung to its tip,
like a speck of dust on the crescent moon

For tearing the demons asunder
For destroying illusion
For making the divine elixir
For raising the earth
Homage to thee, Guardian of the Temple.

Here is an example of a sacred text particular to Gaṇeśa. Some of the concepts are quite obscure and ths might make a suitable object of investigation in your visualisation and meditation.

Gaṇapati Upaniṣad

Auspiciousness to those who hear - thus the Śānti.

1. Oṁ Lam I bow to Gaṇapati.

2. You clearly are the Tattva. You alone are the creator. You alone are the maintainer. You alone are the destroyer. Of all this you are certainly Brahman. You plainly are the essence.

3. Always I speak amṛita. The truth I speak.

4. Protect me. Protect the speakers. Protect the hearers. Protect the givers. Protect the holders. Protect the disciple that repeats. Protect that in the East. Protect that in the South. Protect that in the West. Protect that in the North. Protect that above. Protect that below. Everywhere protect! Protect me everywhere!

5. You are speech. You are consciousness. You are bliss. You are Brahma. You are being-consciousness-bliss. You are the non-dual. You are plainly Brahma. You are knowledge. You are intelligence.

6. You create all this world. You maintain all this world. All this world is seen in You. You are Earth, Water, Air, Fire, Aether. You are beyond the four measures of speech. You are beyond the three Gunas. You are beyond the three bodies. You are beyond the three times. You are always situated in the

Mūlādhāra. You are the being of the three Śaktis. You are always meditated upon by Yogins. You are Brahma, You are Viṣnu, You are Rudra, You are Agni, You are the Vāyu, You are the Sun, You are the Moon, You are Brahma, Bhūr-Bhuvar Svar.

7. 'Ga' the first syllable, after that the first letter, beyond that 'm', then the half-moon all together. Joined with 'oṁ' this is the Mantra form.

8. Letter 'Ga' the first form, letter 'a' the middle form, 'm' the last form. Bīndu the higher form, Nāda the joining together, Saṁhitā the junction. This is the Vidyā of the Lord Gaṇeśa.

9. Gaṇaka is the seer, Nṛcad-gāyatrī the metre, Śrī mahagaṇapati the God. 'Oṁ Gaṇapataye namaḥ'.

10. Let us think of the one-toothed, let us meditate on the crooked trunk, may that tusk direct us.

11. One tusk, four arms, carrying noose and goad, with his hands dispelling fear and granting boons, with a mouse as his banner.

12. Red, with a big belly, with ears like winnowing baskets, wearing red, with limbs smeared with red scent, truly worshipped with red flowers.

13. To the devoted a merciful deva, the Maker of the World, the Prime Cause, who at the beginning of creation was greater than nature and man.

14. He who always meditates thus is a yogin above yogins.

15. Hail to the Lord of Vows, hail to Gaṇapati, hail to the First Lord, hail unto you, to the Big-bellied, One-tusked, Obstacle Destroyer, the Son of Śiva, to the Boon-giver, hail, hail!

16. He who studies this Atharva Śira moves towards Brahma. He is always blissful. He is not bound by any obstacles. He is liberated from the five greater and the five lesser sins. Evening meditation destroys the unmeritous actions of the night. At both evening and morning he is liberated from the bad and he attains Dharma-Artha-Kāma and Mokṣa.

17. This Atharva Shira should not be given to those not pupils. If from delusion a person so does, he is a bad person.

18. He who wants something may accomplish it by 1000 recitations of this. He who sprinkles Gaṇapati with this becomes eloquent. He who recites this on a forth day becomes a knower of Vidya. This is an Atharva saying 'he who moves towards Brahma Vidha is never afraid.' He who worships with fried grains becomes famous and becomes intelligent. He who worships with sweet meat (modaka) gains the desired fruit. He who worships with samit and ghee, by him all is attained, all

is gained by him. He who makes eight Brahmanas understand this becomes like the sun's rays. In a solar eclipe, in a great river or in front of an image having recited this, he gets accomplished in the mantra. He becomes liberated from great obstacles. He is freed from great misfortunes.

Here's another example of a magical text.

Hymn to Gaṇeśa

1. With head bowed, let him unceasingly worship in his mind the God Vināyaka, the Son of Gauri. The refuge of his devotees, for the complete attainment of longevity, amorous desires and wealth.

2. Firstly, as the One with the twisted trunk; secondly, as the One with the single tusk, thirdly, as the One with the fawn-coloured eyes; fourthly, as the One with the elephant's mouth;

3. Fifthly, as the pot-bellied One; sixthly as the monstrous One; seventhly, as the King of Obstacles; eightly, as the smoke-coloured One;

4. Ninethly, as the Moon-Crested One; tenthly, as the Remover of Hindrances; eleventhly, as the Lord of Crowds; twelfthly, as the One with the elephant's face.

5. Whosoever repeats those twelve names at dawn, noon and sunset, for him there is not fear of failure, nay, there is constant good fortune.

6. He who desires knowledge obtains knowledge; he who desires wealth obtains it; he who desires children obtains them; he who desires liberation obtains the way.

7. Whosoever chants the hymn to Gaṇapati reaches their aim in six months, and in a year reaches perfection, on this point there is no doubt.

8. Whosoever makes eight copies of it, and has them distributed to as many Tantriks, reaches knowledge instantaneously, by the grace of Ganesha.

Vināyaka Ahaval (Invocation to Vināyaka)
Cool fragrant lotus feet with anklets tinkling sweet,
gold girdle, flower-soft garment setting off comely hips,
potbelly and big, heavy tusk,
elephant face with the bright, red mark,
five hands, the goad, the noose,
blue body dwelling in the heart;
penulous jaws, four mighty shoulders,
three eyes and the three musk tracks,
two ears, the gold crown gleaming,
the breast aglow with the triple thread,
O Being, bright and beautiful!

wish-yielding elephant,
born of the Master of Mystery in Mount Kailasa,
mouse rider fond of the three famed fruits;
desiring to make me yours this instant
You like a mother have appeared before me
and cut off the delusion of unending births;
stilled my mind in tranquil calm beyond speech
and thought; Clarified my intellect,
plunged me in bliss which is the common ground of Light
and darkness;
boundless beautitude you have given me,
ended all affliction, show the way of grace,
Śiva eternal at the core of sound,
Śiva liṅgam within the heart,
atom within atom, vast beyond all vastness!
sweetness hid in the hardened node,
You have steadied me clear in human form all
besmeared with holy ashes;
added me to the congregation of your servants true and trusty;
made me experience in my heart the inmost meaning
of the five letters;
restored my real state to me, and rule me now,
O Master of Wisdom Vināyaka;
Your feet alone, Your feet alone are my sole refuge
Aum Gaṇeśa, 45-52
(*Translation extracted from Navaratnam*)

Finally

That's more than enough to be going on with. Apart from personal insights it would perhaps be a good thing if you add something to this collection of Gaṇeśa lore. Maybe a version of the myth, a poem, invocation or even a drawing. If you do create something I would be happy to see that.

Love and do what you will'

Bibliography

Avalon, A ed. *Prapañcasara Tantra* Ch 17

Brown, Robert, *Ganesh - Studies of an Asian God*

Courtland, Robert, *Ganesha: Lord of Obstacles, Lord of Beginnings*

Getty, Alice (1936), *Gaṇeśa, a monograph on the elephant faced God*, (OUP).

Grimes, John (1995) *Gaṇapati - Song of the Self*, (SUNY).

Uddasa, Krisnashastri (1892) ed. *Gaṇeśa Purāṇa*, Bombay.

Underhill, M. M .(1921) *The Hindu Religious Year*, (OUP).

Yoroi, K. (1968) *Gaṇeśa-Gīta*, trans. Mouton .

Articles:

Hine, Phil (as Kalkinath), The Destroyer of Obstacles', *Chaos International* No 15,

Notes

1 'The Demon Doctine of Tantra' below.

2 Kalkinath has this as Matāsura - jealousy. Quoted from 'Destroyer of Obstacles' by Kalkinath (Phil Hine) see bibliography. Said to be from Upa *Purāṇa.* I have altered some of the translation. The suffix 'Asura', is sometimes translated 'demon' but you may not wish to follow this line of reasoning.

3 A fortuitous error in the original article of Kalkinath, who omitted one of the eight. Vajrapanimitra of Lila Aropa Zumule (Norway) suggested 'doubt' as an alternative. The sādhaka is invited to substitute their own self chosen demon at this point (īśṭāsura).

3 Contrary to common sense it is not impossible for the moon to be setting just as the sun rises. It is a major twilight and therefore particularly auspicious.

4 We have a piece of family folklore that bans all plaster ornaments from the house. They are thought to be bad luck. I've often wondered if this is common to other parts of Wales and if it is in turn related to some Indo-European folk-memory of the use of plaster rupas in common cults like that of Ganesha.

5 Rendered by Katon Shual from *Prapanchasara Tantra.* Eight is a particularly sacred number in the Ganesha practice.

6 Round sweets particularly favoured by the God.

7 The God is particularly honoured as the Remover of Obstacles

8 In the Gods mythos, he is the miraculous child of Parvati, consort of Shiva. She sets him the task of guarding her sacred bath and of course when he tries to bar Shiva's way, he loses his first human head and later acquires an elephant's instead.

9 Sexual intercourse.

10 In the six Chakra system, an elephant god is described in the muladhara or root chakra. He is a guardian of the earth realm and the entrance to the channels of Kundalini.

11 Turmeric, a magical/medical herb much favoured in Tantrik rites and said to help childbirth, whether of a magical or mundane child.

12 One of five power enjoyments, a code word perhaps for sex without procreation or retention of male or female 'seed'.

13 Shows the *Gaṇeśa*'s affiliation to agricultural deities.

Appendix I

GANESHA CHATURTHI AND GANESHA LEGENDS

Appendix one is a short compilation of mythological material some of it traditional and quite complex on the Internet connected with Ganesha put together for the benefit of the AMOOKOS clan by Anand (ahudli@silver.ucs.indiana.edu).

O Gaṇapati, One with a curved trunk,
a large body, and a brilliance equal to a crore (10 million) suns!
O God, please make all my undertakings free from obstacles always.

Gaṇeśa chaturthi occurs in lunar month of Bhādrapada (August/September) see notes on lunar calendar in appendix. Gaṇeśa or Gaṇapati is an extremely popular God in India. He is called Vighneśvara or Vighnahartā, the Lord of and Destroyer of Obstacles. People mostly worship Him asking for siddhi, success in undertakings, and buddhi, intelligence. He is worshipped before any venture is started. He is also the God of education, knowledge and wisdom, literature, and the fine arts.

Gaṇeśa is also one of the five Gods the worship of whom was popularized by Śaṅkara; the other four are Viṣṇu, Śiva, Devī and Surya. In some cases, a sixth God, Skanda is also worshipped.

The pūja of Gaṇeśa on the Gaṇeśa chaturthi day, extolled in various religious works, is to be performed at noon. A clay image of the God, painted beautifully, is installed on a raised platform. After the usual preliminary rituals, the prāṇapratiṣṭā must be done with the appropriate mantras. This prāṇapratiṣṭā is done for the purpose of invoking the presence of Gaṇeśa into the image. This is followed by the worship with sixteen modes of showing honor, known as ṣoḍaśopacāra. Offering of dūrvā (grass) blades and modaka, a delicacy prepared from rice flour, jaggery, and coconut, is an important part of the pūjā. Usually, 21 dūrvā blades and 21 modakas are offered to the deity, where the number 21 carries a symbolic meaning. The five jnānendriyas or organs of perception, the five karmendriyas or organs of action, the five prāṇas or vital airs, the five bhUtas or elements, and the mind, together comprise 21 parts. The offering of dūrvā blades and the modakas teaches us that we should offer with humility, represented by the dūrvā blades, all the good things in life, represented by the modakas, to God. Gaṇeśa is also offered red flowers, and anointed with a red unguent (rakta candana). The immersion of the image in a body of water is ceremonially performed at the end of the chaturthi vrata, which could be anywhere from a day upto 10 days (Anantachaturdashi) after the Bhādrapada Śukla chaturthi, depending on the customs of the particular family.

I will try to describe the Vedic hymns commonly employed in the Gaṇeśa puja. Ṛg Veda contains the following verses

(Rics) in praise of Ganapati. Ganapati is here identified with Brahmanaspati or Brihaspati, and, sometimes with Indra or Maghavan, Agni and even Rudra.

We invoke You, O Gaṇapati of the ganas (troops),
Who are Brahmanaspati of the brahmas (prayers),
the wisest among the wise,
Who abound in treasure beyond all measure, the most brilliant one.
Do listen to our prayers, come with Your blessings
and assurances of protection into our home, and be seated.

Sit down among the troops (or worshippers), O Gaṇapati, the best sage among the sages. Without You nothing can be done here or far. Accept with honor, O wealthy One, our great and variegated hymns of praise.

By far the most important hymn related to Gaṇeśa is the Gaṇapatyatharva Śīrṣa upaniṣad. This remarkable upaniṣad seeks to equate Gaṇeśavidya with Brahmavidya. For example, it says:

Salutations to You Gaṇapati.
You are indeed the perceptible representation of
'tat tvam asi'.

It is the most widely recited Sanskrit text among devotees of Gaṇeśa, at least in Maharashtra. One can find the entire text of the upanishad on the doorway to the temple hall in the aṣṭavināyaka temple in Rajangaon. Seven other centers of Gaṇeśa worship in Maharashtra are Morgaon, Thevur, Mahad, Lehyadri, Ojhar, Siddha-tek, and Pali. Five of these 8 centers are located in the vicinity of Pune.

Philosophical Significance of Gaṇeśa's form

Gaṇeśa's elephantine head and human body are explained as follows in the Mudgala Purāṇa:

Gaṇeśa's human body representing 'tvam', His elephantine countenance representing 'tat' and their joining together signifies the nondifference of 'tvam' (You) and 'tat' (Brahman). Thus, the body of Gaṇeśa is the visible representation of the highest reality, Brahman, realized from 'tat tvam asi.'

Another explanation has it that Gaṇeśa's head signifies Atman the Highest Reality, while the body below the neck represents mAyA, the principle of phenomenal existence. The Atman's involvement with the world is characterized by the assumption of mind and speech.

Gaṇeśa's ears, which appear like large winnowing baskets, have a philosophical significance too. Just as one uses a winnowing basket to separate grains from dirt, one must use discrimination (viveka) to separate the real (Brahman) from the unreal (māyā) in life. Here the grains stand for Brahman and the dirt signifies māyā. Or, Gaṇeśa's ears indicate that such discrimination between Brahman and māyā is to be gained by taking recourse to Sravaṇa or hearing. Listening to the scriptures from a Guru will lead to proper discrimination and Brahman realization.

Gaṇeśa Legends

Perhaps the most popular story regarding Gaṇeśa's origin is the one derived from the Śiva Purāṇa. Mother Pārvatī once wanted to take a bath and created a boy from the dirt of Her own body, asking him to stand as a guard outside while She bathed. In the meantime Lord Śiva returned home to find a stranger at his door, preventing him from entering. In anger, Śiva cut off the boy's head, upon which Pārvatī was stricken with great grief. In order to console her, Śiva sent out his companions (gaṇa) to fetch the head of anyone found sleeping with his head pointing to the north. They found an elephant sleeping thus and brought back its head. Śiva then attached the elephantine head to the body of the boy and revived him. He named the boy Gaṇapati or commander of His troops, and granted Him a boon that anyone would have to worship Him (Gaṇeśa) before beginning any undertaking.

The Brahma vaivarta Purāṇa narrates a different story regarding the origin of Gaṇapati. Śiva instructed Pārvatī, who wanted to have a son, to observe the puṇyaka vrata for a year to propitiate Viṣṇu.

On completion of the vrata by Pārvatī, it was announced that Kṛṣṇa would incarnate Himself as Her son in every age. Accordingly, Kṛṣṇa was born as a charming infant, delighting Pārvatī who celebrated the event with great enthusiasm. All the Gods arrived to have a look at the baby. But Śani, the son of Sūrya, did not look at him and stared at the ground instead. Upon Pārvatī's questioning regarding his behavior, Śani said that his look would harm the baby. Pārvatī, however, insisted that he should look at the baby. In deference to her wish Śani cast his eyes on the baby. Due to his malevolent glance, the baby's head was severed and flew to Goloka, the abode of Kṛṣṇa. Pārvatī and all the Gods assembled there, including Śiva, were grief-stricken. Thereupon, Viṣnu mounted Garuḍa and rushed to the banks of the Puṣpa-bhadra river and brought back the head of a young elephant. The head of the elephant was joined with the headless body of Pārvatī's son, reviving him. All the Gods blessed Gaṇeśa and wished Him power and prosperity.

Viṣnu blessed Gaṇeśa thus:
O Excellent God! O dear one! May Your pūja be
performed before that of any other God. May You
be situated in all venerable beings and may
You be the best among Yogis. This is My boon to You.

Śiva made Gaṇeśa the leader of his troops (gaṇa), and also gave Him the following boon.

All obstacles, whatever they may be, will be rooted out by worshipping Gaṇeśa, even as diseases are cured by the worship of Sūrya and purity results when Viṣnu is worshiped.

The Syamantaka Jewel

It is said that anyone who looks at the moon on the night of the Gaṇeśa Chaturthi will be falsely charged with theft or a similar crime. If someone inadvertently sees the moon on this night, he/she may remedy the situation by listening to (or reciting) the story of the syamantaka jewel. This story may be found in the Purāṇas such as the Bhagavata and the Viṣnu. Briefly, Satrajit, who secured a jewel syamantaka from Sūrya, did not part with it even when Kṛṣṇa the Lord of Dvaraka, asked for it saying it would be safe with Him. Prasena, the brother of Satrajit went out hunting wearing the jewel but was killed by a lion. Jambavan of Rāmāyana fame killed the lion and gave it to his son to play with. When Prasena did not return, Satrajit falsely accused Kṛṣṇa of killing Prasena for the sake of the jewel. Kṛṣṇa, in order to remove the stain on His reputation, set out in search of the jewel and found it in Jambavan's cave, with his child. Jambavan attacked Kṛṣṇa thinking Him to be an intruder who had come to take away the jewel. They fought each other for 28 days, when Jambavan, his whole body terribly weakened from the hammering of Kṛṣṇa's fists, finally recognized Him as Rāma.

I now know You.
You are the life in all creatures, virility,

grit and strength. You are Viṣnu, the Primeval Lord,
All-prevailing, the Supreme Lord (of the worlds).

(Bhagavata 10.56.26)

and

He Who built a bridge (across the ocean) that is a standing monument to His fame, set Lanka ablaze, and with His arrows severed the heads of Rākṣasas, which fell to the ground.

As repentance for his having fought Kṛṣṇa, Jambavan gave Kṛṣṇa the jewel and also his daughter Jambavati in marriage. Kṛṣṇa returned to Dvaraka with Jambavati and the jewel, and returned it Satrajit, who in turn repented for his false accusation. He promptly offered to give Kṛṣṇa the jewel and his daughter Satyabhama in marriage. Kṛṣṇa accepted Satyabhama as His wife but did not accept the jewel.

In the event one is not even able to listen to or read the story, the following mantra may be recited holding some water in the palm of the right hand. The water is then to be sipped.

A lion killed Prasena; the lion was killed by Jambavan.
Don't cry, O dear child! This syamantaka jewel is yours.

A Gaṇeśa stotra from the Narada Purāṇa

One should bow the head and offer obeisance before the son of Gauri, Vināyaka, whose abode is the devotees, and remember Him always for the purpose of obtaining longevity, and desired objects (prosperity).

Now the twelve names of Gaṇeśa are mentioned.

Finally

After Lord Gaṇeśa has been duly worshipped according to Vedic methods, an Arati or waving of lights is performed. Sometimes the song sung during this ceremony is in the regional language. It is customary to sing some Sanskrit verses after the song, these end:

Hare rāma hare rāma rāma rāma hare hare |
Hare Kṛṣṇa hare Kṛṣṇa Kṛṣṇa Kṛṣṇa hare hare ||
SrI Kṛṣṇārpaṇamastu ||

Appendix II The 'Demon' Doctrine and the roots of Tantra

In order to understand the Tantrik experience you have to know what came before. You have to go back to the roots of Hindu orthodoxy in what is known as Vedic religion. For those who don't know, the Vedas are four manuals of ritual - Ṛig, Sāman, Yajur and Atharva. The Ṛig described the rhythm, the Sāman the music, the Yajur the contents and the Arthava the correspondences.[1] The *Arthava Veda* includes a vast amount of medical and sympathetic Magick. The Vedas are some of the oldest writings on ritual (not Magick) in the world. The bulk of them were systematised in about 1500 BCE, although some of the material goes back before that. Fascinating as this material is from an historical point of view, as a religious or magical practice it has little place in the modern world. The *Vedas* encapsulate the religious practices of a particular group of people known as the Aryans. The Vedic Aryans were a warlike and expansionist people, who had many branches in their family tree, including ancient Iran, in which some of the Vedas were actually written.[2]

The Vedic Aryans brought the Iron age to India, advancing from the north west through all parts. The possession of iron weapons gave them the technological edge with which to subdue the indigenous tribes. However this process did not occur without a fight, and for many centuries the cult of the warrior reigned supreme. Vedic religious rites were therefore often very martial in flavour. The function of the caste of priests was to facilitate the warriors and hasten the subjugation of what to them were barbarous tribes. The basic fire altar was actually shaped like a giant bird, wings outstretched in flight in the direction of the east - the unconquered land. Each year at the great fire rituals, the altar would be built further and further to the east. The awesome fire deity Agni, said to have legs made of iron, was the patron. Fire which has been so beneficent to humanity is also the agent of battle and destruction.

Steadily the land was subdued and the violence of the warrior caste became less welcome and the priestly caste schemed to moderate it and at the same time increase their own status. It was perhaps at this point that the original recipe for the powerful psychoactive drug Soma was lost, maybe deliberately as part of the process of pacification.

It is said that the first casualty of war is truth. And in the mayhem of the Vedic period it was common practice to typify the enemy as 'barbarian' and their deities as 'demons'. These demons were themselves lorded over by former Aryan deities that had not travelled well into the new lands and had become the anti-Gods. These are the Asuras.

There is nothing particularly sinister about the name Asura. In the earliest strata of the *Vedas* it meant divine being and was applied equally to the Gods, including some like Indra, who is not considered particularly demonic. The term Asura is cognate with Ahura, as in the Ahura Mazda of Zoroastrianism. In fact the supreme demons in later Vedic religion were the supreme Gods of another time and place before the separation of the Indo-European people into distinct groups. Chief amongst the Asuras was Varuna, a noble austere deity. All this tends to underline the fact that there is no such thing as absolute evil. As H.P. Blavatsky said with some real insight, 'Good to some is evil to other.'

The Asuras are the Elder Gods. In fact 'Sura', the later word for Gods is a linguistic fiction accomplished by merely dropping the initial 'a'.

It is my contention that Tantrism is, partly at least, a revival of the doctrine of the Asuras. In this instance this includes the Vedic and non-Vedic original deities of the culture that existed in India before the coming of the Aryans. As part of this argument, it is significant that Dattātreya, the originator of the Tantrik rites, was said to be the teacher of the Asuras.[3]

The First Tantrik

Dattātreya is said to be the originator of Tantrik rites - i.e. he was the first Tantrik. It is difficult to say whether he was ever a human being. Like many other figures from the past such as Hermes Trismegistos or Imhotep, his deeds were so famous he became deified. Before you rush out and buy one of the printed books ascribed to Dattātreya a word of warning. Like many interesting figures in the history of Hinduism his image has been given a coat of whitewash. Most of the published translations of his known writings concentrate on the orthodox aspects of his philosophy. For example *Dattātreya: The Way and the Goal* by J.C.W. Bahadur (Combe Springs 1982) includes the *Dattātreya Upaniṣad*, the *Jīvanmukta Gīta* and the *Avadhūta Gīta.* These texts are full of wisdom although it shows only one side of Dattātreya, that of traditional guru. Even so there are gems here such as:

> There is neither scripture, nor worlds, nor Gods nor sacrifices, no classes nor stages of life, neither race nor caste, neither the way of smoke nor the path of the flame. Brahman is the Highest Reality.[4]

This hints at Dattātreya's anti-establishment character which is further underlined by:

> If all the commandments are negated, if everything is realized to be the highest Self, if Mind is free from dualistic ideas, and if the talk of luck and so on are abandoned, then in the case of that aspirant there is neither purity nor impurity, nor the distinction of sex. [5]

and again

> There need be no concern whether the Guru happens to be a boy or a man or one who is found gratified with pleasures of sense or seems obstinate, whether he be a slave or a householder. For who will reject a gem for the mere reason that it is found in an impure place.[6]

We must add girl and woman to the list of potential Gurus, bearing in mind the original primacy of the female line within Tantrism. Otherwise the tone is radical, rejecting social classes and rigidly orthodox ideas on ritual purity which discriminates according to race and sex etc. However the substance of these books is still rather austere and only hints at anything recognisably Tantrik.

Dattātreya the Magician is buried under layer upon layer of denial. The first big obstacle is the fact that left-hand path texts are largely untranslated and often not easily available even in Sanskrit. The three main left-hand-path Tantras of Dattātreya are the *Gandharva-Tantra*, the Dattātreya-*Tantra* and the *Paraśūrama*. The *Gandharva* mentioned in the first of these is a Nature spirit representing the sense of smell. The Dattātreya-*Tantra* describes the quintessential six acts of Tantrik Magick: Pacification, Subjugation, Immobilization, Spreading Discord, Driving Away and Liquidation. The final text describes typically Tantrik worship of the great Śakti Tripurā.

The Tantrik image of Dattātreya is very rarely seen in sculpture or painting. I have a lithograph bought at my neighbourhood bookshop, but the image is anaemic and boring. However a very rare cave sculpture of the twelfth century shows Dattātreya with one of his four hands clasping his erect phallus (Narmadā Caves, Broach, Gujurat). There is also a Dattātreya piṭha, a hill sacred to the Tantrik Guru near Mysore (Chikmaghlur district) although over the years the Guru/guardianship of the shrine has passed into Muslim hands.[7] His image is almost always shown with three heads as he sits cross-legged in front of his eternal fire pit. At each of the four directions a large dog keeps guard. It is common to interpret the three heads as *Trimurti* - the three faced representation of Brahman: the Creator God, Viṣnu the Preserver and Śiva the Destroyer. This makes Dattātreya a nice neat icon of the three main deities of classical Hinduism. Nevertheless I think this interpretation is probably a later rationalization of what is essentially an primeval non-Vedic deity. In a similar way, the four dogs are explained as representing the four Vedas (see above), an odd symbol for such holy books, given that dogs are normally regarded as ritually impure. Oddly enough the triple-headed male deity, shown naked and surrounded by four beasts is one of the oldest representations of the divine that has survived from antiquity. It appeared on the seal-stones found in the remains of the indigenous and pre-Aryan Indus Valley civilization. This culture remains still as a mystery to us. Its script has never been deciphered, although artefacts from Mesopotamia and Minoan Crete have been found in its abandoned cities.

In modern times it is not uncommon to represent Dattātreya merely by a pair of sandals. Some writers have tried to link Dattātreya with the Egyptian God *Thoth*. Another interesting link with the ancient Near-East is the constellation the Dog (Canis Major) which has four stars, like the four footed dog itself or even the four dogs of Dattātreya.

When Dattātreya was born, he did what came naturally to him as an avatar of Viṣnu and sank to the bottom of a lake. Ancient mythology tells us that Viṣnu in his first and therefore most creative incarnation took the form of a fish. This motif of divine knowledge passing to humanity from the denizens of a lake or river is one that recurs again and again in Tantrism, and indeed Hinduism. Prospective disciples assembled around this lake and bade Dattātreya rise up and instruct them in the Mysteries. He duly did so, appearing naked in sexual union with a woman. The orthodox interpret this as a test of the disciple's resolve. Rather like the ordeal of the 'demon' Crowley, they must swallow their deep shock and revulsion at the sight of their guru having it off and be patient. Later he rises to the surface with a jug of wine and proceeds to get drunk. Again, is this an ordeal or a subtle message? At the third request he says that as a drinker of wine and one who is attached to women, it is futile to ask a boon or help from such a man without character and who has no knowledge of the way. This time they persist and he accepts those who have persisted through the 'ordeal' as students and enlightens them. Perhaps this is one possible interpretation of the three heads of Dattātreya, enjoying his love, another is intoxicated and the third form is a synthesis of the other two.

Given the large measure of the fantastic to be found in tales of Dattātreya, it may seem rash to ascribe to him actual earthly status. His name means 'gift to Ātri' , which means he was one of three sons given to Ātri in return for some service to the Gods. Ātri; (The Devourer), was in India, a famous shaman or Seer, whose exploits are recorded in the Purāṇas, ancient 'histories' of the Vedic people. Worship of Dattātreya continues to the present and he is particularly popular amongst the Nāthas sect. The Yogic philosopher Gorakhnāth, tangled with him several times. Some texts speak of the nine Nāthas (Navanāthas) who sit around his sacred fire-pit. These may be symbols of the nine orifices of the body through which the world is encountered: eyes, nostrils, ears, mouth, urethra/ vagina, anus. According to Alain Daniélou, in his wonderful source book of Hindu mythology *Hindu Polytheism*,[8] Dattātreya was the teacher of the Asuras. Some of what he taught them may be found in an early India 'Gnostic' text known in academic circles as the Sāṁkhya Kārikā (the Gnostic verses). The distinguished Sanskrit scholar F. Edgerton[9] suggests that 'Sāṁkhya' could be translated as Gnosticism, which literally means the way of knowledge. This philosophy forms the basis of the Yoga Sūtras (q.v.), and of the alchemical and medical schools.[10] It is therefore the direct ancestor of Tantrism.

The Gnostic philosophy will be discussed in details below. One of its important sources is by Indian standards, a short text called the Sāṁkhya Kārikā (the Gnostic Verses). The source of this doctrine was the great Vedic Sage Kapila.[11] Kapila's first pupil was an Āsuri - a so-called anti-God. Although quite an obscure text it has been translated many times into English, one of the best by S. S. S. Shastri, (Madras 1935) or J. Davies (London 1881). The second verse of this document[12] says that:

> The Vedic means of terminating misery is fruitless, it is verily linked with impurity, destruction and excess.

Once again then we come back to the criticism of the Vedic way, primarily because of the association of its rituals with violence and excess. Perhaps an example of one of these rites will underline the point. A celebrated sacrifice of the Vedic Aryans was the horse sacrifice (aśvameda). The prologue to this took over a year, and began when a specially consecrated horse was released and then tracked by a heavily armed band of warriors. The horse would naturally wander over the lands of rival tribes. Warriors from this tribe were then challenged to return the horse with a ransom or do battle. This cycle of challenge and bloodshed continued for a year after which the horse was captured and led back to the original hearth to be sacrificed amid great brutality. It is said that the tribal queen engaged in ritual intercourse with the dying animal and was drenched in blood as its life ebbed away.[13]

Such spectacles obviously sickened many of the more progressive minds of the day and the reaction is clear in the text mentioned above. In one legend a band of warriors chase the horse into the underworld, where they disturb Kapila himself. Kapila is so incensed he curses them and burning them to ashes.

Are the Tantriks Moral?

I belong to a modern Tantrik sodality that traces its roots back to Dattātreya. This Order is known in the West as the Kaula Nātha Clan which includes AMOOKOS[14] and it is one of the first Tantrik sodalities to acknowledge an affinity between its ideas and those of *Thelema* and Aleister Crowley.[15] I recently heard someone say that modern Magicians no longer have room for talk of morality. I think he meant that the whole agenda for this kind of discussion has been set by the orthodox and conservative religions 'of the book' and perhaps we should find some other way of setting out our ideas.

However ethics was part of the ancient Pagan philosophy where it was the study of character and manners. It strikes me that even the most free-minded have some code or values by which they abide and hope other people will. People who say that there is no need to even discuss these questions, are, I think deluding themselves. A person who has never examined their own ethical code is not free from it, the very opposite, they merely don't know where their real boundaries lie.

When thinking about my own system of ethics I started by looking at metaphysical theories, a fruitful area, so one would think. Unfortunately, the results of attempts to analyse good and bad in terms of metaphysical principles, such as the Hindu law of Karma or Plato's eternal forms have resulted in bad laws. It is my contention that John Stuart Mill's Utilitarian model is still the most tenable; perhaps with some modification of later empirical moralists such as William James. It is clear from a close examination of their work that neither philosopher denies the validity of other realities. They assert rather that these magical realms are the object of mystical speculation and cannot be analysed by natural concepts. They do not attempt to bridge this unbridgeable divide, which has frustrated thinkers for so long. They attempt to short-circuit the argument by adopting a pragmatic approach. What people mean by 'good' is pleasure or happiness. An *ethical* act should therefore be one that gives the greatest good to the greatest number. Ones actions on balance should create more pleasure than pain. It follows from this that our actions should not cause unnecessary suffering. It strikes me that most magical systems can live quite happily within this framework, it is, after all based on something called the *pleasure principle*. How else could the proto Tantriks or Gnostics have criticized the barbaric sacrifices of the Vedic Aryans?

At some point the reader is sure to realize that the tantriks have been known to practice blood sacrifice. Even in the modern day, there still may be a case for this in certain extreme circumstances. It is because I have thought about a moral code I can say that killing can be justified. Those who claim to be amoral are often found to fudge this issue. After all, people eat sacrificed animals in their kitchens everyday day of the week. Even so, one has to apply the equation - is the suffering of the animal, however small, really necessary? Is the aim really large enough to justify the means taken? Crowley wrote that a sacrificed animal:

> must not be too large; the amount of energy disengaged is almost unimaginably great, and out of all proportion to the strength of the animal.[16]

In a footnote he gives as an example the sacrifice of a bull which 'is sufficient for a large number of people; hence it's common in public ceremonies; i.e. for a whole kingdom.' In my opinion, there is hardly any magical result that cannot be achieved by alternatives to sacrificing an animal. Furthermore, modern Magick has largely moved away from attempts to invoke spirits to visible manifestation, which is traditionally said to require a great deal of energy. How about sacrificing a large denomination bank note - try burning one in your ritual, it's surprising how much emotion you have tied up in it. Or try making something, like a pot or other artefact and breaking that in the ritual. An apparently deserted Kālī temple I visited on the outskirts of Khajaraho was full of such 'sacrifices'. The magician's own blood or semen is another common sacrifice.[17]

In perhaps the most misunderstood passage in Crowley he recommends the sacrifice of a 'male child of perfect innocence and high intelligence.'[18] The footnote elaborates that he had made this particular sacrifice an average of 150 times each year. The 'male child' is of course Crowley's own semen. Ejaculation, or its equivalent is truly a sacrifice from the point of view of classical Yoga, which places great emphasis on retention of semen. It is undoubtedly a sacrifice, albeit temporary, of the body's physical resources, and most are tired immediately afterwards. However the sacrifice is almost always rewarded and the body, in my opinion, gains new strength from the sacrifice, perhaps as a blessing of the deity. By way of contrast, the mean retainer of semen, is often mentally drained . Plotinus, the neo-Platonic philosopher, had a method for distinguishing good spirits from evil spirits. Bad spirits may make you feel good in their presence but later you may feel that you've been abused. Good spirits may make you feel awe-struck at the time but you feel refreshed and purified afterwards. Perhaps we can apply similar criteria to the way we feel after a 'sacrifice' of our body's energy.

Notes

1 Bṛihadāranyaka Upaniṣad 4.1.2

2 'Ireland' or 'Eire' is said by philologists also to be related to the word 'Aryan'.

3 See Gaṇeśa and the Gajasuras - see Kalkinath's article on Gan* for names.

4 Dattātreya: *The Way and the Goal* by J. C. W. Bahadur (Combe Springs 1982) .Avadhūta Gīta 39.

5 Same work 39

6 Same work II.1

7 A. Bharati, *The Tantric Tradition* (Rider, 1980) p. 186.

8 Recently republished as *Gods and Myths of India* (Inner Traditions 1991) p. 181.

9 F. Edgerton *The Beginnings of Indian Philosophy* p.36

10 See Chris Morgan, *Medicine of the Gods*, (Mandrake of Oxford 1994).

11 There is an interesting passage in the Mahābhārata in which Kapilā is said to be the wife of Asuri, and that she passed on the doctrine to *her* adopted son whilst suckling him. See *MBh* Śānti *Parvan* Ch. 218.

12 Which along with the *Serpent Power* can be compared to the Kabbalistic *Sepher Yetzirah.*

13 Giraldus the Welshmen, a British monk, whose family were but a few generations from being Pagan Celts, described a similar sacrifice in Ireland. The main difference was that in Ireland it appears that the King and not the Queen, was the human partner in this mystical marriage. This idea is also found in the marriage of the horse goddess Rhiannon to Pwyll Lord of Dyfed, as recounted in first branch of the *Mabinogi.*

14 The Arcane and Magical Knights of Shamballa.

15 Thelema is a Greek word meaning Will, usually interpreted as Free[will].

16 *Magick* p. 222.

17 In Eastern physiology, 'semen' could apply equally to men and women. Interestingly several recent reports talk of female ejaculation, not of semen but of a build-up of sexual fluids from glands within the vagina. Of the several women I have asked about this they say it is not a regular event but occurs now and again after sustained stimulation of the tissues around the urethra. This may be borne out by an important new study of female sexual anatomy called *Eve's Secrets* by J. Lowndes-Sevely. She proposed among other things that the area around the urethra in women is the equivalent of the male prostate or ejaculatory organ.

18 *Magick* p. 219.

Appendix III
Tales of Hindu Devilry: Vikram & the *Vetāla*

In 1987 Shantidevi and myself visited Shri Mahendranāth (Dadaji), the now departed Guru of the East-West Tantrik Order AMOOKOS, in his retreat at Shamballa Tampovane just outside Ahmedabad. We exchanged gifts and he gave me an inconsequential booklet entitled *King Vikram and the Ghost.* After we had left I packed this away with other things and didn't look at it for several years when a chance conversation drew it to my attention.

It was in fact a reprint of C.H. Tawney's translation of *Vetālapañcaviṁśati*, - 'Twenty-five vampire tales' - a classic of Tantrik folklore. At the end of the formal part of the ritual, when the Gods have been invoked, the elixir shared, the ritual combat complete, then, as in times past, is a good moment for story telling. And what better tale to recall than one of these twenty-five.

In an earlier chapter I referred to the high tradition of Indian literature and the 'little' or folk tradition in which so much Tantrik material finds its roots. The *Vetālapañcaviṁśati* is part of this folk tradition. As so often when describing things Indian one must have recourse to superlatives. Indian literature has a vast wealth of narrative prose. The orthodox side of this is to be found in the Purāṇas or ancient legends such as the Mahābhārata and Rāmāyana. These may have been favoured for recital during the build up to the notorious horse sacrifice.

Separate from this heterodox tradition is the *Ocean of Story* or more accurately the Kathā-Sarit-Sāgara - *Ocean of the Streams of Story*. A great collection of tales that is likened to an ocean because the streams of all stories flow into it. But as if the mind needs any more boggling the *Ocean of Story* is itself a rendering of a greater lost original called the *Blooms of the Great Story* (Bṛihat-Kathā-Mañjari).

Perhaps it would help if I explained that all Indian art mirrors life in its extreme intricacy - to it the ideals of Platonic simplicity are alien. This can be seen in the sensory overload incurred whenever one gazes upon an Hindu temple. Every available inch seems to be covered with images of the utmost complexity and from every aspect of life. In the temple at Halebid in South India, only one tiny segment is left uncarved - and this is done to underline the fact that despite the thousands of carvings, the temple is an incomplete representation of the world!

But the Indian mind is not so very different to our own and sections of the *Ocean of Story* were circulated in smaller, more manageable bits. Two particular sections have an independent existence from the *Ocean of Story* - the *Pañcatantra* and the Vetāla-Pañcaviṁśati.

The Pañcatantra

The first of these is not a Tantrik work despite its name. Remember that the term 'Tantra' has the mundane meaning of 'treatise'. Pañcatantra or 'five treatises' is in fact a collection of animal stories each of which teach some aspect of everyday ethics; for instance when the weak band together they can often achieve more that the strong. From its emergence approximately two thousand years ago, the *Pancatantra* has been translated into almost every language. Many other sets of animal stories such as Aesop's *Fables*, Apuleius' *Golden Ass*, Bocaccios' *Decameron* and La Fontaine's *Fables* - all are almost certainly related to the Pañcatantra stories.

Take for instance the Welsh legend of Llewellyn and his dog Gerlert. Local Pembrokeshire folklore says that the Preseli mountains are the reified remains of the wrongly accused dog Gerlert. In his struggle to guard Llewellyn's child from a wolf, the dog and the baby's cradle is covered in blood. When Llewellyn returns and sees the bloodstained crib he makes the over hasty assumption that Gerlert has gone mad and killed his child. He hurls his deadly javelin at Gerlert. Moments later he discovers the corpse of the wolf and the baby - alive and well. His remorse reminds us not to make hasty assumptions. The story is identical in almost all details with the frame story of the fifth book of the Pañcatantra, although the protagonists in that story are a cobra and a mongoose.

Vikram and Vetāla

Vetāla-Pañcaviṁśati is thoroughly rooted in the world of Witchcraft and Tantrik Magick. Both are described in a manner far removed from the medieval descriptions of the Western Witch-hunts. It is obvious that the narrators had a fascination, indeed a love/hate relation with the Witches and Magicians.

King Vikram, who is one of the central characters of the collection of these twenty-five tales of Indian devilry, is encountered in the first or so-called 'frame' story. His name means 'Son of Heroism' and he is a legendary King, very like King Arthur. He ruled over a golden age that still bears his name and is used to set the date on Indian birth certificates. He patronized all the arts and sciences. Interestingly his father suffered the same fate as Lucius in the *Golden Ass* and was cursed to assume the form of an ass during the day.

The other central character is the Vetāla. Richard Burton in his rendering of this book into English suggested that a Vetāla is a vampire and this has been followed by many subsequent editors. The Vetāla is neither a vampire nor a ghost. As the stories make clear a Vetāla is a special class of demon, outwardly ghoulish but in fact benevolent towards humanity.

It is interesting that the lost original from which these tales are said to be drawn was written in the language of demons -called 'Paiśāci' by the grammarians. I would remind the reader of what I wrote in another appendix concerning the possible demonic origin of Tantra. 'Paiśāci' may just mean 'rough dialect' of the common folk and is, according to some authorities, a dialect related to the Romany tongue. There is some convincing linguistic evidence that the Romanies migrated from Northern India, in approximately the third century before the common era. Whatever way one looks at it 'Paiśāci' is a lost 'demonic' language, which only survives in stories such as Vetāla-Pañcaviṁśati.

Indian physicians were often called upon to deal with cases of demonic possession and the various kinds of demon are therefore described in some detail within their texts[1] . Their medical expertise at 'Bhūta-Vidyā', literally 'Knowledge of Spirits' may seem at odds with the overall materialistic tone of Äyurveda medical education. In the main it was only in perinatal deaths and also certain intractable kinds of mental illness that the blame was laid on demonic possession. Some modern commentators have even seen in this a rudimentary form of psychiatry.

Demonic possession is called 'graha' in Sanskrit and there are said to be nine classes of possessing demon. The standard list begins with possession by the Gods (Devas), which shows that possession by a God can be undesirable in many circumstances. The other seven in order are Asuras (Elder Gods: see appendix two); Gandharvas or nature spirits; Yakṣas or ancient nature spirits; Pitṛis or ghosts of departed ancestors; Bhūjañgas or serpent spirits; Rākṣasas or ferocious ones and finally Piśācas: demons. A person possessed by the last of these displays the following bad personality traits: haughtiness, emaciation, rough language and behaviour, extreme uncleanliness, restive, voracious appetite, fondness for cold water and lonely places such as the night forest, graveyards etc., where they weep and wail incessantly.

The demons are able to take possession when a ritual is badly performed or the correct observances forgotten. The Piśāca demons are the only ones that can be driven out by force and without killing the victim. All the others must be propitiated or they will kill the possessed person. This is further evidence that this class of demon is somehow beyond the pale of orthodox society and can therefore be freely insulted if they refuse to leave after propitiation has been tried. They are in this respect like the demonic entities invoked in Goetic Magick that are firmly licensed to depart by the magician and threatened if they refuse to go.

Various incenses and potions are recommended to drive them out. Cooked or uncooked meat is another favourite way of tempting a demon to leave a victim of possession. Grahas or possession in children is much more serious and with alarming regularity the incident ended in death. Mythologically these demons are said to have been created by the Gods to guard the new born God Kārttikeya or Skanda. Paradoxically these same possessing entities can turn on the child. Unlike the adult versions, these are personified as fearful Goddesses, for example Śakuni the bird Goddess so important to Tantrik rites, or in two instances as male Gods. They must be propitiated very carefully with the appropriate rites described in the medical texts of Suśruta.[2]

Indian philosophy divides all matter into three fundamental particles or guṇas called sattvas, rājas and tamas - which can perhaps be translated simply as essence, energy and substance.[3] These are thought of as real particles and all matter is composed of them in various permutations. Mind is particularly rich in the three gunas and of them, disturbance of rājas and tamas is said to be the most productive of mental imbalance and not surprisingly we find that all classes of demons are predominantly rājas and/or tamas. Two thirds of the demons have no essence (sattva) at all - they are in effect automata. Some examples of this hierarchy of demons and the possible personality traits they inspire is shown in the following table:

The Äyurvedic Personality Archetypes		
Sattva Mind	Rājas Mind	Tamasa Mind
Brāhma Type (godly)	Asura (ruthless)	Pāśva (bestial)
Ṛśi (sagely)	Paiśāci (Manic depressive)	Matsya (fishy)
Indra (authoritative)	Sarpa4 (reptilian/deceitful)	Vānaspatya (vegetative)
Yama (restrained)	Preta (morbid)	
Varuna (courageous)	Śakuni (officious)	
Kuvera (generous)		
Gandharva (ecstatic)		

The Piśācas are associated with rājas amongst the guṇas . This energetic and feminine aspect of our personality when out of balance leads in this system to manic depression or melancholia. In our own tradition enlightened melancholy is a magical state that can lead to liberation.

Some of these personality types are associated with the lunar parts of Indian astrology. The Brahman type with the day of the full-moon; the Ṛiṣi and Asura with dusk and dawn; the Rākṣasas with the moon's dark fortnight and the Preta with its bright fortnight.

One last piece of folklore before returning to our story - there are in the Hindu tradition said to be eight types of marriage - one for each of the classes of possessing entities. Gandharva marriage occurs very commonly in story and happens when the partners are so intoxicated with each other that they marry without informing any relatives or without any formal ceremony. It is said that a Gandharva inspires such unions because of its peculiar affinity with the sense of smell, and hence eroticism in general. The eighth class of marriage inspired by the Piśācas is but a hair's breadth from rape. The erstwhile partner is tricked into union whilst asleep or by being placed into a compromising situation from which marriage is the only antidote.

I'm assuming that the Vetāla of our story is one of those class of Piśācas demons given in the table. The standard dictionaries have no ready etymology for this word, a fact I always find exciting because it suggests a folk origin. Vetala's are often seen on the sides of Nepalese temples, shown with a horrific countenance and wearing a yellow skirt. Perhaps the creature became popularized in Nepal when the story cycle was translated into Nepalese in the eleventh century by the poet and folklorist Kshemendra (I say folklorist because he is also responsible for an encyclopaedia of customs composed in 1037).

The Vetāla was once a normal person who overheard Śiva telling Pārvatī a collection of stories for her ears only. He was cursed to remain a Vetāla until such time as he could find someone clever enough to answer the riddles set in each story. There is in fact a whole Tantra on Vetāla Magick itself embedded in a huge compendium of Tantrik ritual compiled by Krishnānanda.[5] This is called *Tantrasara,* one of several works bearing the same title, the most famous being the work of Abhinavagupta, who was an adept of the right hand path.

The Frame Story[6]

And so to the story:

Once upon a time there was a mighty King called Vikram. People came from far and wide to offer him presents as a token of their loyalty. And then one day a naked holy man walked into his audience room and offered him a single fruit. The King accepted the humble gift with as much grace as he would any other gift of greater value. At the end of the audience he handed it to his steward thinking he would eat it but in fact he placed it through a window in an abandoned part of the treasury. And from that day on the naked holy man was a regular visitor to the righteous King's audience room and each time he brought the same gift - a single fruit picked from the wild trees in the forest.

Until one day the King took a fancy to give the fruit to one of the semi-tame monkeys that roamed about the place and then an odd thing happened. The monkey bit the fruit and then immediately threw it down. Glowing inside the broken body of the fruit they saw a wonderful diamond of the highest value. And when they looked in the place where the other fruits had been thrown they found a large pile of similar gems.

And so the King resolved to question the holy man the next time he came. The holy man said that the jewel was as nothing and that if the King would help him drive away the demons that plagued his forest ritual, then he would give him a gift greater than any so far seen.

And so it was agreed that King Vikram would meet the holy man at midnight at a desolate spot in the centre of a large forest cremation ground. Nervously the King, armed with his finest sword, walked through the fearful and desolate place to a lonely ritual fire. He saw the holy man and began to wonder at what manner of ritual he was celebrating at this hour. But before he could question him, he was reminded of his oath and sent on a quest to the loneliest and blackest part of the cremation ground where he would find a fresh corpse hanging from a tree. Bound by his oath he went there and climbed the tree and brought down the corpse with great difficulty. Sweating with the effort he laid it down ready to heave it up on to his shoulder for the walk back to the holy man's ritual circle. And in his mind he resolved to question closely the supposed holy man as to the nature of his activities. But even before he had struggled but a few yards he felt the corpse move. His heart in his mouth King Vikram steeled himself, took a deep breath and resolved to hang onto the corpse and fulfil his mission. For he had seen many a corpse on the battle field and knew that this was surely a dead body when he brought it down from the tree.

On his grandmother's knee he had heard tales of the miraculous Vetāla spirit that took hold of the body after death and could be very mischievous to the living. He must, he knew, get the possessed corpse to the ritual fire as soon as possible.

But then the Vetāla began to speak. "Righteous King Vikram, the night is black and cold and the way long. Let me tell a tale to shorten the journey."

"Be silent", yelled Vikram as he quickened his pace, but still the Vetala demon went on:

The Fifth Story

There was once a handsome washerman, who whilst on a sacred pilgrimage saw a beautiful woman and instantly fell in love with her. He mooned away for some time not knowing what to do. But eventually his loving parents realized his predicament and arranged a marriage to the liking of all involved. And great was the happiness of the loving couple and both families.

And then his brother-in-law, who was a zealous devotee of Kālī, suggested that they should visit Kāmarūpa, the chief temple of the terrible Goddess, and show respect to the one at whose festival the star crossed lovers had first met.

But when they got to the temple of Kālī the brother-in-law remembered that they had no offerings to make to the awesome Goddess and advised that they should not enter the holy of holies. But the bridegroom was flushed with the power of love and thought he would go in anyway and meditate at the feet of Kālī. And during that meditation he was seized with a passion for the Goddess and resolved to offer everything he had to Kālī, including his own life. And he took up a sword that had been left there as an offering, and fixing his hair to the bell rope that hung above the shrine, he cut off his own head with one stroke, and his body fell to one side.[7]

The brother-in-law hearing the bell was filled with foreboding ran into the shrine and saw the terrible carnage. Such was his sorrow at loosing his new friend and the bridegroom and his dread at causing his beloved sister pain by bearing such bad news, he resolved to repeat the sacrifice. And indeed the bell soon rang a second time.

The beautiful bride was by this time worried to distraction and she forced herself to go into the dreaded shrine and there the terrible sight of the decapitated bodies of her brother and lover she did see.

And with one piteous cry to the Goddess she resolved to join them, taking up a nearby creeper she tied it about her neck in order to hang herself. But even as she began to stretch her neck the awesome Goddess appeared to her and said "enough of this carnage, the piety of your family is not in question, ask what ever you wish of me, for I am moved to pity."

And the widowed bride asked only for the lives of her lover and brother and was duly instructed to place the heads back on the shoulders and all would be well. But her eyes streaming with tears she mistakenly placed the wrong head on the wrong shoulders. And when the bodies of the two men revived she saw her mistake.

"Well" said the Vetāla to the righteous King who had all the time he was walking been listening intently to the demon's tale. "Well" said the Vetāla, "answer me this, which of those two men is now the rightful bridegroom?"

"That is an evil tale demon spirit, but according to Kaula & Tantrik lore, the head and not the heart as is sometimes said, is the true seat of consciousness. Whichever body bears the head of her husband, that shall be her rightful lover."

And saying this the righteous King Vikram, renewed his grip on the Vetāla, knowing that if his answer to the riddle was correct the demon would attempt to escape. And sure enough the corpse possessed by a Vetāla spirit slipped through his hands and flew off into the air, screaming through the forest back to its place in the tree.

There are twenty-five such tales, occupying the whole night and through them Vikram is eventually initiated into higher knowledge and learns how to avoid the tricky fate awaiting him when he does eventually get the demon back to the ritual.

Notes

1 See Chris Morgan, *Medicine of the Gods* (Mandrake of Oxford 1994)

2 Suśruta Saṁhitā, English translation by G.D. Singhal et al, *Medical & Psychiatric Considerations in Ancient Indian Surgery* (otherwise known as *Uttara-Tantra*) ch 37sq.

3 See Chris Morgan, *Medicine of the Gods*, p. 10 and, *Ancient Indian Gnosticism* (Mandrake of Oxford) forthcoming.

4 *Sarpa-dosa* is the curse of baresness caused by harming a snake. See Bharati, *The Tantric Tradition* p. 94

5 There is an account of his life in Sircar, *The Shakta Pithas* (1948) p. 74sq. See also Pal, P. (1981) *Hindu Religion and Iconography According to the Tantrasara.* Los Angeles, for a selection of useful material.

6 I have adapted this version of the story from C.H. Tawney's English translation of Somadeva's *Kathā-sarit-sāgara.* Various editions are available including one from Jaico Publising House.

7 Elgood, R. (2005) *Hindu Arms and Ritual: Arms and Armour from India* (1400 - 1865) (Chicago University Press). Shows devotees of Bahdrakali with the swords used in rites of self-decapitation.

Invocation of Kuṇḍalini

by Krisna Murugan

Beautiful like a chain of lightning
Fine like a (lotus) fibre,
Shining in the minds of the sages
Subtle are you;
The awakener of pure knowledge
The embodiment of all bliss,
Whose nature is pure consciousness
Guardian of the way
The doorway to the creator
It shines in your mouth
Entrance to the region of bliss
Sprinkled by the elixir of immortality
Untie this knot
Serpent, ruler of knots
Unhinge your jaw
And open your mouth
The way of Suṣumṇā

You are Goddess of earth too
Surrounded by eight shining mountains
Indra protects you with his mighty arms
And his great, elephant mount
Like a vast mountain of smoke
Stands by
Seven too are the mountains
Secret kula name of your places
Pārvatī of the tribe

Yellow are you
Lam, your mantra
You who maintain all beings

By inspiration and expiration
You sleep over the body linga
kuṇḍalini
The world bewilderer
Gently you cover the door with your own mouth
Like the spiral of the conch shell
Your shining snake like form
Goes three and half times around Śiva
Your murmur is of love sick bees
You inspire poetry
You make sigils (bandha)
Your snake form flows through all language
I meditate upon Kuṇḍalini
Self-chosen Goddess
Of manifest and unmanifest sound

A young girl are you
In the full bloom of youth
With fine breasts
Adorned with all adornments
Like the full moon,
Red in colour
With restless eyes like a snake

Your seat is a lion
I worship you in a triangle
I offer water to your water
Blood to your blood
Semen to your semen
Accept what I offer
The white and the red
Fluids mixed together
Transform them,
Find the rasa in them
Enter again the root of me
Bhujaṅgī , Kuṇḍalini, Tripurā-sundarī

Appendix V
The Serpent Power

Being the ṢAṬ Cakra Nirūpana and Pādukā Paṣcaka Translated by Arthur Avalon (Sir John Woodroffe).

It is important to acquire an authentic Tantrik version of the Cakra system, for this reason it is recommended that you study at least the final section of Woodroffe's book, the long introduction may be safely omitted at this stage.

This translation first saw the light of day in 1919 and has been in print pretty well ever since. Unfortunately it appeared too late to be of any influence on the Theosophical Society, whose (often offbeat) ideas on this subject have influenced people much more. The primary concern of the work is the investigation of the six cakra system or the centres of energy in our psychic anatomy. Although one could be excused for missing the point due to the fact that well over two thirds of the book is devoted to Arthur Avalon's own introduction to Kuṇḍalini Yoga, running in fact to over three hundred pages! This introduction whilst authoritative, is heavy going and abounds on enough technicalities to turn off even the most committed. This introduction in turn has its own introduction, written against a backdrop of Theosophical thought which Avalon is at pains to correct.

These difficulties aside, this text is an essential manual for the magician working with Tantrik ideas and if one scans the worthy introduction and goes to the essence, one finds a crucial investigation into the six Cakras.

To clear one point, it may strike the reader that many recent books speak of seven or even eight Cakras, ie: anus, genitals, stomach, heart, throat, 'third eye' and brain. These are *rough* approximations of Sanskrit Mūlādhāra, Svādhisṭhāna, Maṇīpūra, Anāhata, Viśuddha, Ājña and Sahasrāra Cakras. However, in this system the brain (Sahasrāra) is not called a Cakra proper but an experience or synthetic quality of the other six. There are of course other Cakra systems, as described in my book *Sexual Magick* (Mandrake 1989) and one must beware any dogmatism on this point. Aleister Crowley may well have had access to one of these other systems, perhaps from the *Śiva Saṁhitā*, when he wrote the Yogic poem, reproduced at the beginning of *Magick in Theory & Practice* (Penguin edition).

The Serpent Power is pure Magick and needs many hours of careful meditation and study to distil its full import. The author was a Shaivite called Pūrṇānanda who wrote in about 1571AD a large digest of Tantrik ritual. This investigation of the six Cakras is merely a small part, in fact chapter six, but as with many celebrated texts, for example the Bhagavad Gītā, it has taken on an independent existence. This monograph on Kuṇḍalini is heavily influenced by early Tantrik exponents such as Matsyendranātha (qv). Ideally when studying this text one needs a competent guide or Guru, but in its absence the body is a good guide and I suggest that one works through each Cakra and its connections in sequence, perhaps writing out and simplifying the meditational image so that it can be clearly visualized in the correct part of the body. Here is an example of what I mean.

Begin the meditation in your normal manner with banishing etc. Then sit in your comfortable posture and focus on the root Cakra (Mūlādhāra). It is attached to the mouth of the spinal column and placed below the genitals and above the anus. Imagine it as a flower (lotus or rose) with four petals of crimson hue. Its head hanging downwards. On each petals someone has written a letter of the alphabet in shining gold ink: Va, Ṣa, Śa, and Sa. Within the four petals is a square representing Earth, surrounded by a circle of eight shining spears. It is of a shining yellow colour and beautiful like lightning. The syllable Lam, is just visible in yellow ink written in the same square. If you look hard at Lam you will see a God, mounted on one of the finest of elephants. On his lap he carries the Child-Creator, resplendent like a young Sun.

The guardian of this Cakra is the Goddess Ḍākinī, her arms shine with beauty and her eyes are brilliant red. She is resplendent like the lustre of many suns rising at once and the same time. She is the carrier of the revelation of the ever pure intelligence.

Near the open end of the spinal column there constantly shines the beautiful luminous and soft lightning like triangle called Kāmarūpa. It is here that the love God dwells. Inside the triangle is the Śiva-liṅgam, beautiful like molten gold with his head downwards. He is revealed by knowledge and meditation and is of the shape and colour of a new leaf. As the cool rays of lightning and the full moon charm, so does his beauty. The God dwells happily here as in his mountain home. Over the liṅgam shines the sleeping Kuṇḍalini, fine as the fibre of a flowerstalk.

She is the world bewilderer, gently covering the mouth of the spinal column with her own. Like the spiral of a conch shell, her shining snake-like form goes three and half times round Śiva and her lustre is as that of a strong flash of lightning. Her sweet murmur is like the indistinct hum of love mad bees. She produces melodious poetry and all other compositions in prose and poetry, in sequence and otherwise, in Sanskrit and other languages. It is she who maintains all the beings of the world by means of inspiration and expiration and shines there at the bottommost flower, like a chain of brilliant lights.

Within Kuṇḍalini is the awakener of eternal knowledge. She is the omnipotent Kālī who is wonderfully skilful to create, and is more subtle than the subtlest. She is the receptacle of that continuous stream of the elixir of life (Amṛita) which flows from the eternal bliss.

Appendix VI The Kaulajñana-Nirṇaya of the School of Matsyendranātha

This text is edited with exhaustive introduction by P.C. Bagchi, with English Translation available from Michael Magee (Prachya Prakasha: Varanasi 1986).

This published version is 700 verses in 24 chapters, the first of which, though incomplete, is ascribed to Matsyendranātha, the founder of the Kaula practice. Several important subjects to the adept are treated in a manner not always easy to follow due to the preponderance of obscure technical expressions. This is probably a text for someone with an initiated knowledge and rewards close study. The introduction by P.C. Bagchi is very authoritative and runs to 90 pages. It provides a thorough introduction to the history and philosophy of the Nātha (Sovereign) sect of Tantriks still active and organised in the UK today.

The text is set out in the traditional manner of a dialogue between Devī and Bhairava. The main topic is the particular type of Yoga practiced by the Kaulas. The adept is recommended to realise the cosmic process of creation and dissolution with his own body. Particular importance is given to the colour red, the mantra Haṁsa and the concept of Svecchācara or following one's own Will. Also emphasised are the three Śakti: Desire, Knowledge and Action. In this tradition the Guru is particularly important and is viewed as an embodiment of Śiva, and can therefore help others on the path to liberation.

Chapter One has only two surviving verses but seems to have concerned the heat of the five fires.

Chapter Two completes this theme of the ultimate source of the World. Visualisation of the five fires is an important Tantrik technique.

Chapter Three introduced the concept of the body liṅgam, or Yantra which is known more commonly as the Śrī Yantra. Ie the primal correspondence between the arts of the body and corresponding parts of the cosmos.

Several chapters deal with the supernatural powers that are available to the adept. This includes the 'six-acts' and those for combating old age, disease and death.

Chapter 8 concerns different Śaktis and their worship. A ritual is described in which one eats fish, meat, alcohol and sexual intercourse.

Chapter 9 deals with the line of innumerable Gurus and Yoginīs.

Chaper 10 describes some Bijas (seed Mantras) and their position on the Śrī Yantra and the body. Six Cakras of the body are also described.

Chapter 11 deals with ritual food.

Chapter 14 with Kaula Yoga.

Later chapters are main sources of Kaula rituals and Yogi exercises of various sorts including the terifying Savasadhana or meditation sitting on a corpse.

Appendix VII The Yoga Sūtras of Patañjali

(based on the edition of Rama Prasada with commentary of Vyasa and gloss of Vācaspatimiśra, (Allahabad 1910) SBH Vol IV.)

0. Introduction

The Yoga Sūtras (hereafter referred to as YS) were written sometime around the beginning of the Christian era. The sometime called 'Sūtra' period runs from approximately 2nd century BC to 2nd century AD). There are approximately 194 aphorisms or Sūtras, divided between four chapters. A Sūtras is an extremely compressed summary of a particularly doctrine. Sūtras texts were composed around this time, partly in response to the onslaught of Buddhist argument. They aim to provide a concise statement of doctrine, capable of answering all points of controversy. There are no superfluous words in a Sūtras text. Thus subsequent commentaries, which often have a status at least as great as the orignal Sūtras, make a practice of analysing each individual word.

The division into four chapters or 'pādas' (literary feet) appears to be an archetypal way to construct a magical text. The four parts have different significance:

i. Samādhi Pāda: Yoga for the best qualified people, capable of the yogic, one-pointed trance.

ii. Kriya Pāda: Yoga of Action, for medium-ranged needing practical instruction as to the means of Yoga.

iii. Siddhi or Vibhuti Pāda: Common to all, the attainments of Yoga.

iv. Kaivalya Pāda, Yoga of absolute independence.

The YS are the practical half of the ancient Indian Gnostic philosophy, which goes under the title of 'Sāṁkhya'. This is one of the oldest systems of Indian philosophy, predating even Buddhism. Its ideas permeate all areas of subsequent schools of religion and philosophy. The basic tenet of Sāṁkhya-Yoga is that the world is divided into two principles of matter and spirit. It is not possible to say which of these has precedence over the other. These two principles are often referred to metaphorically as male (Puruṣa) and female (Prakṛti). The ideas of Sāṁkhya-Yoga and the YS are the bedrock of the later Tantrik schools of Magick, Hindu and Buddhist.

Patañjali is a legendary figure in Indian history. He is said to have gotten his name because of his miraculous birth. Legend has it that he fell from the sky in the form of a serpent, from the 'añjali', or praying hands or 'mudrā' of a female ascetic. He is also credited with the authorship of a medical text (perhaps the Caraka Saṁhitā, whose author also has serpent connections), as well as a grammatical text. Thus the following invocation is to be read before all study of the YS:

I bow with praying hands to Patañjali,
Who was superior to all sages;
Who purifies the Mind of its impurities by Yoga
The voice of its impurities by his grammar
The physical body of its impurities by his Medicine.

I suspect that a manuscript text would have an opening dedication to Gaṇeśa as patron of learning, but this is not given in the printed edition and neither is there a Sanskrit colophon (by-line). Here's a few lines to give you the flavour:

1.1. Atha Yoga-Anushāsanam
Atha = now, benedictory particle
Yoga = work, Magick, practice
anushāsanam = revised text.

Patañjali is not the creator of the Yoga practice. Vācaspati says that according to Yājñavalkya, the creator of the Yoga practice was Hiraṇayagarbha. This is the name of a Vedic deity, whose name means literally 'Golden Egg'. He is then the cosmic egg from which all creation proceeds.

1.2. Yogaś citta-vṛtti-nirodhaḥ

citta = thought/mind
vṛtti = disturbances, turmoil, modification,
nirodhaḥ = non-sprouting, restraint

Note that not 'all' modifications are restraints. Yoga is about restraint of most mental modification, ideally all but one. Thus Yoga is a kind of concentration that arizes from one-pointed meditation.

Mind in this system is a singular thing. Yoga is the practical side of Sāṁkhya Gnosticism. This philosophy divides the world into Puruṣa/Prakṛti; simply put Man and Woman (vṛtti is feminine noun). Mind (Manas, Citta) is part of Nature not Spirit, although it is closer to it, than other modifications of matter. All matter in this system is composed of three qualities or guṇas. They combine like primary colours to produce secondary and tertiary 'colours'. Mind is a secondary formation. In order to purify Mind, one must concentrate on one of the gunas in particular and try to forget the rest. Sattvas is the purest and many 'God' orientated people (Divyas) would concentrate on this. The Tantriks (Virya) would focus on Rājas: energy, a word also related to menstrual blood. Only an animal type (paśu), would remain focused on the most dense of these, Tamas or very earthly things.

Appendix VIII The Grammar of Tantra

The first scientific grammar was written in about the second century by Pāṇini, an almost legendary figure in Indian history. It was a study of the Sanskrit language and designed to preserve the actual sound of the language. Think for a moment how much one takes for granted the use of an English alphabet of a mere twenty-six letters. We are often told that good pronounciation equals correct emphasis or is it emphāsis? How much more important is correct pronounciation in a magical context, when some believe the vibration must be appropriate to achieve the desired results. Grammar grew out of a religious philosophy concerning the origin of the universe as sound. The earliest Veda texts are called 'Śruti' because they were actually heard by the Vedic Shamans. Later texts are 'memories', and are thus known as 'Smṛti', remembered by 'smart' Brahmins. The Sanskrit language encapsulates an esoteric philosophy, echoed in the Western magical tradition with its reliance on grimoires or magical grammars.

Appendix IX
TheVāmakeśvarīmatam

We see the continuation of opposition to 'Vedic ways' in full blown Tantrik texts as the Vāmakeśvarīmatam. This text is not mentioned by Abinavagupta, the extremely thorough ancient historian of Tantra who lived in C1000AD. It is often assumed from this that the text cannot be older than this date. It is an important text of more than secondary importance. Vāmakeśvarīmatam means 'the doctrine of the Queen of the Left Hand Path'. It is a Tantra of the Śrī Vidyā school, a text of particular importance to worshipers of the primordial Goddess. Śrī Vidyā is concerned with the Mysteries of the fifteen syllable Mantra:

Ka-e-ī-la-hrīṁ, Ha-sa-ka-ha-la-hrīṁ, Sa-ka-la-hrīṁ.

It is worth seeing this written in Sanskrit even if the meaning is obscure, as it has the quality of a sigil. Each letter has a particular correspondence and the three phrases together make a Mystery of sexual Magick.

The Vāmakeśvarīmatam is actually an umbrella title for two works, one called *The Yoginī Hṛdaya*: 'The Heart of the Yoginī' and the other a short work which deals with the tradition of the sixteen eternal Goddesses. The latter is the one discussed below. Both texts deal in great detail with the symbolism and meaning of the celebrated Śrī Yantra.

Śrī is yet another name for the primal Goddess. Her name means 'Fortune' and she is one of the oldest Goddesses of the tradition. Śrī features in Vedic texts and was said to have been one of the Asuras or Elder Gods. She is in fact one of few Asuras to make the transition from the age of the 'Titans' to the new pantheon. This further underlines the contention that Tantra is a revival of the worship of the Asuras: the antigods or demons.

The text begins with a litany of the Goddess, who is said to be made of mantra. The magical connection of speech and word is further underlined by the devotion made to the Goddess by the avian Garuḍa and several other deities of speech and sound.

Sound is the primal menstrum in Tantra, thus all Magick is largely to do with the correct vibration of sounds. The Vedic texts are actually called 'Śruti' or heard texts. They are the record of the divine musick of the spheres as set down by ancient shamans.

Orthodox Brahmins give this a fundamentalist twist. They claim that the Vedic texts were not composed by humans, merely recorded by them. Therefore the Vedic injunctions must be followed in all respects as they are the literal words of God. This ultra-orthodox philosophy, called mīmāṁsā: 'the investigation', had its good and bad sides. It probably led to a train of thought that developed the first scientific grammars in world history. The motive for this was a conservative desire to preserve the supposed sound of the Vedic texts. On the negative side it valorised the Vedic sacrifice full of blood and guts and a class system which excluded the working classes (Śūdras) from important religious rites.

The Tantriks tackled the fundamentalists on their own ground, pointing out certain ridiculous aspects of the literalist view.

The Tantriks discounted the orthodox claim that revelation was at an end and that the Vedas were a closed book. Thus when the Tantriks say the Goddess is language they are claiming a new inner contact with the divine principle that supersedes that of the fundamentalists.

The main part of the Vāmakeśvarīmatam describes the construction of a mystical diagram familiar to us as the Śrī Yantra. The structure of this book is very similar to grimoires of the western tradition such as the *Key of Solomon*. In both cases a complex mystical diagram is described and the mode of construction and activation set forth. The planetary and elemental correspondences are listed, everything necessary to bring the image to life, including the invocation using the breath, in which flower petals are individually charged and dropped on the image. This latter practice is reminiscent of the creation of the flower maiden Blodweth, as told in the Mabinogion. The Śrī Yantra is now alive.

The Red Rite

The dhyāna or meditational image of the Goddess is described at I.113-133. After a long description of her beauty we are told she appears clothed in red garments, holding a noose and a goad. She sits on a red lotus and is adorned with red gems. She has four arms and three eyes and she holds five arrows and a bow. The operator too, must utilize red 'correspondences' if he or she is to invoke this aspect of the deity.

The reward of all this hard work is then given including the ability to perform the six acts or and other miraculous powers. Most prominent amongst these is the power to attract women. The Vāmakeśvarīmatam is a traditional text and doesn't quite make it into the modern world. Despite slight male bias it still reveals the ancient power of the Yoginīs, the female spirit, whose powerful kiss the practitioner craves as he or she calls her to the circle of Magick. The text goes on to describe other powers gained by the Red Rite including construction of protective amulets and how to subdue and eliminate enemies etc.

The White Rite

Interestingly the earlier parts of this grimoire concern what has become known as results Magick. Chapter four, verse 21 onwards describes the White Rite. In this rite all the correspondences are white, ie the operator wears white clothes and offers white flowers etc. The results of this are gnostic and include knowledge of medicine, something particularly prized by the Tantriks. It also bestows knowledge of the six philosophies of India: Sāṁkhya—Gnosticism; Yoga—Meditation; Nyāya—Logic; Vaiśeṣika—Atomism; Mīmāṁsā—Vedic Investigation and Vedānta—Monism. The Goddess Tripura is a muse who inspires the operator with poetry and all of the sixty-four Arts, which are hers.

The Third or Mixed Rite

The third and final part of the text, starting from chapter five is the highest initiation. It describes how the operator becomes like the Goddess Tripura and is able to truly act according to his or her own will. The operator is liberated from time and death.

The three rites together comprise the three Shaktis Kriya (Action); Jñāna (Knowledge) and Icchā (Will), said to be symbolized by the three points of a triangle in the Śrī Yantra.

In this small book is outlined all that is necessary for the accomplishment of Śākta rites although full utilization needs a great deal of study, practice and probably the benefit of an experienced guide. Even so it is a remarkable ancient Tantrik text.

Oracles

The Tantrik Knuckle Bone Oracles Theory and Practice

By Mogg Morgan

111	112	113	114	121	122	123	124
131	132	133	134	141	142	143	144
211	212	213	214	221	222	223	224
231	232	233	234	241	242	243	244
331	332	333	334	321	322	323	324
311	314	313	314	341	342	343	344
411	412	413	414	421	422	423	424
431	432	433	434	441	442	443	444

Śrī Gaṇeśaya namaḥ

Namo Gaṇeśāya vighneśvarāya

Introduction

This book is a rendering of the Pāśaka Kevalī, or doctrine of divination by dice. The translator Hoernle says the text is still found in India as a manuscript or occasionally as a printed Hindi book.[1] The author is usually said to be Ṛṣi Garga who was believed to be the archetypal astronomer/astrologer of the ancient Vedic age.

The Bower Manuscript

The Bower Manuscript is one of the oldest physically surviving Indian manuscripts. Apart from inscriptions on stone or metal, most Indian texts were written on perishable materials such as birch bark or specially treated banana leaves. The volatile nature of these materials necessitated the recopying of any ancient text after a regular term, usually every hundred years. The texts that comprise the Bower Manuscript bypassed this process and remained buried for at least the last 2000 years. It was discovered in 1890 at Kuchar in Kashmir (41° 42' North, 80° 33' East), buried under the ruins of a Buddhist stupa. Perhaps this is a real example of a Buddhist *terma*, whereby sacred ideas were supposedly placed in 'time-capsules' for discovery by later generations in need of their secret doctrines.

The definitive edition of the Bower Manuscript was published by the Archaeological Survey of India (Calcutta 1893). It is edited by the eminent Indologist and medical historian F.Rudolf Hoernle and comprises a facsimile of the original leaves, a Nāgarī transcript, romanized transliteration and

English translation with notes. The original is housed in the Bodleian Library, Oxford.[2] It actually consists of seven manuscripts, five of them on medical subjects. Hoernle dated it on the basis of its Gupta script to the fourth century of our era.

Some of its fifty one leaves are out of order, but Hoernle says that there is no reason to believe that this was their original condition. This latter point is significant because it indicates whether the text was used on the basis of its contents or as some kind of medical fetish. It is the work of no less than four scribes, one of whom needed numerous amendments by a later colleague. Parts IV and V are concerned with the ancient art of cubomancy or divination by dice, and it is these that I have rendered in the core of this appendice. The contents of the other manuscripts are given in a footnote.[3]

Divination and Medicine

The discovery of the Pāśaka amongst other medical manuscripts, indicates that there was a close connection between divination and medicine. The ancient Āyurvedic medical system used quite a lot of observations that are nowadays frowned upon by modern physicians. However it is my view that if used with wisdom then the use of divination can be a valuable extension of the healing Art. Āyurveda made creative use of dream analysis as a variety of early or prodromal symptoms of disease. (For more on Āyurveda, see my book *Medicine of the Gods.*)

The second, incomplete divinatory manuscript, reproduced in the appendices, reverses this and has bodily symptoms such for example blisters or boils, as indication of the truth of the oracles. In my experience the first part of a divination, consists of the diviner telling the querent things about their present situation, that they already know. If the diviner gets this right, then the querent usually has more confidence in the part of the oracle that concerns future or unknown events.

By the Eighteenth Century, the analysis of dreams had reached a very high degree of sophistication in the Indian intellectual tradition. In the verses I used from a later text to fill the gaps in the more ancient oracle, it is interesting to note the observation of special dreams to indicate that the prediction is beginning to manifest. There has been so much attention given in recent years to the phenomenon of lucid dreaming, that the observation of significant dreams is in danger of being overlooked. Significant dreams are periodic dreams, often in full colour, sometimes disturbing and always remembered, either upon waking, later during the day, or sometimes weeks later. Significant dreams, have occured most frequently in my life, at times of passage, when my life was approaching a threshold or crisis. For example, I have on record significant dreams from the months leading up to my departure from school, when I was obviosuly concerned about what I would do in terms of career or occupation.

I also had dreams connected with what is sometimes called a totem animal or perhaps alter ego. It is a common practice among magicians to seek out such totems. Some commentators believe these animal totems should come naturally in the course of life, and need not be 'forced' by undertaking, what for us might be, artificial or contrived 'visual quests'. Magicians, rightly or wrongly, tend to value spontaneity in such matters. I have a friend who was trampled by a horse and now views this as magically significant. Her life now is very much dedicated to the Magick of the horse. I have another friend who was repeatedly bitten by a venomous spider whilst asleep. This prompted a nightmare that woke her in time to save her life. She now feel that the spider is an important personal totem. For me, one of my totem animals attacked, not in real life but in a dream. I recently heard it said that in places such as Britain or Europe, most of us live in cities and have very little daily contact with animals, certainly not the close proximity of our ancestors of only a few generations back. However when I look around the streets where I live, I am surrounded by animals of one sort or another, perhaps I take them for granted. There are spiders, moths, bugs everywhere, woodlice in the toilet, voles, mice, hedgehogs and birds of many varieties in our tiny garden. I have a domesticated cat, and see dogs, horses, deer (some wild) almost every week. But not surprisingly, the totem animal that attacked in my adolescent dream, was a domestic dog. Well partly so, part Alsatian, half wolf. I still bear the scars.

How Can Divination Work?

Good question. Divination is a kind of Magick. It seems to me that there are two possible ways in which Magick works. Take Crowley's definition, 'Magick is the art and science of causing change in conformity with will.' Crowley avoids the issue of ontology - realism or idealism. Perhaps his definition works regardless of the ontology. Take for sample a materialist view, the world has substance. (Notes: some kinds of Hindu philosophy maintain that the world has no substance or essence. It is rather kinetic, a collection of moving relationships). This implies that the practitioner of Magick is able to 'change this substance' by the use of will, which is part of the mind. But in some sense, Mind is itself immaterial - how can something immaterial like Mind, effect matter without the mediation of other agencies? In order for me to open a door, I may begin with the desire to open the door, but bring into play my whole physical body, nerves, muscles etc. This process involves fairly well understood laws of Nature which do not appear magical. To try to open the door by any other means, for instance by ordering the door to open, would appear to contradict these laws.

Conventional wisdom tells us that will power alone cannot open a solid door, or perhaps only in certain rare and spontaneous conditions that are occasionally documented in parapsychological literature. To all intents and purposes it cannot be done, or so it seems. Perhaps we should look at a more tractible example, instead of a gross thing like willing a door to open. How about attempting to move a very small object, perhaps even the smallest object we know of. Is the human will alone capable of moving a single molecule or atom?

It must be so, how else is thinking possible. For although the mind is immaterial, it is nevertheless bounded by matter. It appears to be localised in the human nervous system or within the body, excepting perhaps that there may be occasional expansions or variations to this limiting in the case of dreaming, out of the body experiences and the like. The mind is a paradox, it is immaterial and material at the same time. The most common metaphor is of a ghostly thing inhabiting the human organism. Whatever the answer to the riddle of the relationship between mind and matter, it must be constantly willing matter to move. Marek Kohn in an article entitled 'Sex and the Brain' (*Guardian Weekend Magazine*, August 5th 1995 pp. 13-18) discusses some new experiments on the brain using magnetic resonance imaging. (MRI). This technique highlights activity in the brain by measuring blood flow. The part of the right hemisphere of a subject's brain asked to complete a similar task, 'lit up', showing that the task was being processed in that region. The 'lighting up' was in fact a measurement of increased blood flow as the vessels in that part of the brain dilated. So thinking and brain structure are closely related, but where did the instruction for the blood vessels to dilate emanate from? When we think of a colour, the blood vessels in part of our brain dilate, perhaps waking one or two brain cells or neurons from their slumber and releasing the memory. Without knowing how this was done, we have willed a small number of cells in the circulatory system to move, and this by the exercise of human will. Unlike more gross phenomena, it is near impossible to fake this movement of a tiny number of cells.

If it is conceded that Mind has this ability to make small changes in its physical environment, then there at least is any answer to those enemies of Magick who say that it rests on an impossible relationship between Mind and Matter. It plainly does not. The problem for Magick lies in quantity rather than quality of action. That I can slow my heart rate down may not be impressive, someone once told me that they would only be convinced of the power of Magick if I could demonstrate God-like powers, such as slowing the spin of the Earth!

Preposterous, well maybe I can do that. The secret lies in divination. The point is that the mind is a very sensitive instrument. It can make small changes in its environment which, if well timed, lead to bigger changes. It follows that it is also very sensitive to change. It may be that it can be made more sensitive to minute clues of impending gross changes and thus predict them. Take for instance the example of astrology. That the personality of a tiny unborn baby is somehow related to the movements of the planets seems unlikely. It is more likely that things develop the other way round, that the unborn baby is sensitive to the position of the planets. They do not make his or her personality, that is determined by other things. But the mind of a baby may be sensitive to certain planetary configurations. Within limits, the fetus can determine the timing of its own birth, not the month but perhaps the time of day. Birth itself may well be triggered by a hormone secreted by the foetus, in effect Mind says, 'now I will be born', the hormone passes into the mother bloodstream and begins the process.

Method of use

The mode of throwing the divination die (pāso) is as follows. When the die is wanted for an oracle (Skr Śakuna[4]), it must be thrown three times, and the first cast counted as hundred. Thus, if one pip falls, it counts as 100; if two pips 200; if three pips fall in the first cast, 300 and if four pips 400.

Next the die is thrown for a second time. Then of the pips that fall, one counts as 10, two pips as 20; three pips as 30 and four pips as 40. In the same way the cast of the third time must be understood. Finally the hundred in the first throw and the figures of the second and third throw must be placed together. Whatever, (combined) figure results, upon that the oracle must be pronounced. Thus if first one falls, next two, and next at the third throw, three fall, then it is the (combined) figure 123, one hundred and twenty three. Similarly, if at the first (cast) two fall, next one falls, next three falls, the result is the figure 213, two hundred and thirteen. This is the correct manner of proceeding.[5]

It is clear that the type of die used is of the elongated kind, rather than the more familiar regular cubes.[6] This type is known as a talus, astragalas or knucklebone, because of its resemblance to that piece of anatomy. The four throwing sides are marked by pips, and the two blank ends are 'joined' with the two presiding servitors of the divination - the Mantanga (elephant, perhaps Gaṇeśa or according to Hoernle, the Caṇḍāla or outcaste? man) and the Kumbhakārā (the potter woman).

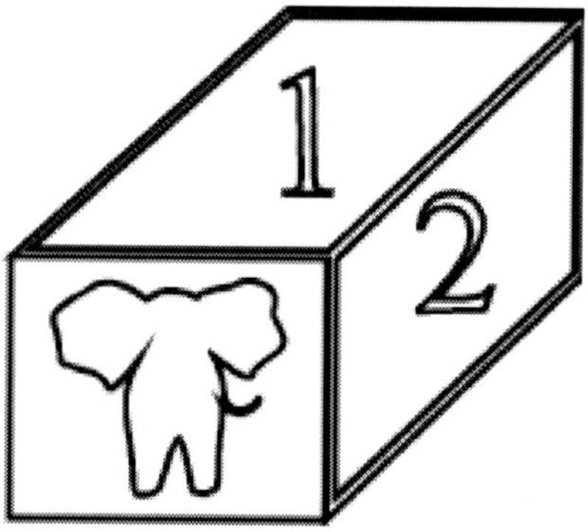

Invocation to be said before casting the dice.

Salutation to Nandi-Rudra Iśvara!

Salutation to the Ācāryas!

Salutation to Iśvara!

Salutation to Māṇībhadra!

Salutation to all Yaksas!

Salutation to all Devas.

To Śiva Salutation!

To Śaṣṭi Salutation!

To Prajāpati Salutation!

To Rudra Salutation!

Salutation to Vaiśrāvaṇa!

Salutation to the Marutas!

Salutation!

Let the dice fall for the purpose of the present object (i.e. of divination)!

Hili! Hili!

Let them fall as befits the union of Kumbhakārī the potter woman and, Mātanga[7] the outcast man! By the truth of all the Siddhas, by the truth of all Schools, by their truth and true consensus let Śiva declare what is lost and preserves, peace and trouble, gain and loss, victory and defeat, svāhā!

On the holy Nārāyaṇa, the tutelary Devata, and on the Ṛṣis rests the truth of the oracle, the truth of the process of divination. Let the dice fall openly! svaha! Let the truth be seen! The efficacy of magical formulas and medical herbs and prognostics is far from untruth. In praise of the Devata Viṣnu.

Key for identifying the throws				
Last Throw = First two throws below	**1**	**2**	**3**	**4**
11	4	38	37	32
12	39	30	52	64
13	36	61	22	54
14	33	49	57	12
21	40	31	60	48
22	29	3	28	25
23	62	27	19	46
24	50	24	43	9
31	35	63	21	56
32	59	26	18	41
33	20	17	2	15
34	53	45	14	7
41	34	51	55	11
42	47	23	44	10
43	58	42	16	6
44	13	8	5	1

Example: You throw the dice three times, yielding 1 on the first throw, two on second and four on third - 124. Look up 12 row in bold characters on the left and then follow your finger across the page to the fourth row. The number in the box is the number to look up in the oracle ie: 64

Meanings of the various throws:

1. The Mantra (Chaṇṭayāṇṭa): 444

   Salutation! Janādana is well-pleased with you who art an excellent man. All your enemies are killed. What you desire, that shall be done.[8]

2. The Nine (Navikki): 333:

   You experience neither sorrow nor fatigue; nor hast you any fear of either high or low: ....you will receive.

3. The Turban (A Paṭṭabandha): 222:

   Even in the midst of the full enjoyment of all desires, your happiness engenders molestation; but as soon as it arises, may God allay your fears.

4. Kālī breaking through (Kālaviddhi): 111:

   Your intelligence is at fault; [....]; the under-taking which you contemplate will be fruitless.

The Three Obstacles or Curses (Śāpaṭa)

5. The first Śāpaṭa: 443:

   You will quickly be delivered from all diseases; or, again, you will obtain happiness; *but* in the result; you will not attain anything either very great or very small.

6. The second Śāpaṭa: 434:

   I see a terrible effort *against those* with whom you are in conflict, *but* I see the work to be fruitless on account of which you have consulted the oracle.

7. The third Śāpaṭa: 344:

   You are contemplating a meeting, *but* the fair one does not join you; your body is heated *with desire*, *but* you shall obtain no enjoyment.

The Three Choices (Vṛśas)

8. The first Vṛśas: 442:

   Whatever there is in your house, cattle, grain and money, you should distribute among the spiritual people;* your advancement is *then* near at hand.

9. The second Vṛśas: 244:

   You are planning a meeting, and your beloved is far away; but the fulfilment of all your desires will come to pass in a not-very-long time.

10. The third Vṛśas: 424:

    You will suffer grievous bondage, but you will regain your place; you will have your reward and will also have peace.

The Three Illusions or Dilemmas (Kūṭas)

11. The first Kūṭas: 414:

    There is a quarrel with the government, hence there is a cessation of law and order; *but* you have obtained an advantage; therefore you should surely observe law and order.

12. The second Kūṭas: 144:

    Unsteady is your present place; there is neither comfort, nor progress in friendships; *but* you will get relief even if you are held fast by the Gods: there is no doubt about it.

13. The third Kūṭas: 441:

    There is comfort; there is no fear; I see here also triumph; you will enjoy [men and] women accomplished in the arts of love; from nowhere hast thou anything to fear.

The Three Garlands (Mālīs)

14. The first Mālīs: 343:

    The enjoyment of pleasure and wealth, and the fulfilment of all desires come together; they will, in a very short time, be yours, and that for ever.

15. The second Mālīs: 334:

    You think this to be a valuable thing, *viz.*, happiness that promotes good-will; by patience you will attain that great object but not if you are impatient.

16. The third Mālīs: 433:

    This is considered a great object by you; *but* there is a much better object than that: a safe journey into foreign parts and a *safe* return to one's friends.

The Three Rogues (Viṭis)

17. The first Viṭis: 332:

    You have never too much trouble, and are clever in your business; you will not suffer any misfortune, nor will you be triumphed over by your adversaries.

18. The second Viṭis: 323:

    You will not meet the object of your advantage, and will meet with disappointment; *but* go quickly to another place, *and* you will obtain very great happiness.

19. The third Viṭis: 233:

    I see your purpose; it is with reference to obtaining the first place;[10] it will come to pass for you as surely as the word of Maruta.[11]

The Three Cyclops (Kaṇas)

20. The first Kaṇa: 331:

    The safety of your person, profit and wealth are within your grasp, and your prosperity is at hand as sure as the word of Maruta.[12]

21. The second Kaṇa: 313:

    You expect health and abundant power: there is no doubt about it; you will certainly obtain prosperity, and abundant pleasures also.

22. The third Kaṇa: 133:

    You speak untruths sometimes, *and* you always show ill-will to your friends; *but* wait, *and* by the favour of the Gods your prosperity will come to pass.

The Three Servants (Preśyās)

23. The first Preśyās: 422:

    If you desire knowledge or [anything],[13] but sit idly at home, you will be altogether unsuccessful.

24. The second Preśyās: 242:

    The thing that you have thought of, [that course of action], it will not accomplish that business with regard to which you enquirest.

25. The third Preśyās: 224:

    The speech which you have meditated, that will be the cause of wealth: there will be acquisition of wealth for you in a very short time: there is not doubt about it.

The Three Outcomes (Sajās)

26. The first Sajās: 322:

    You will triumph over all your enemies, but you will have one powerful adversary; you will obtain the first place, *but* afterwards you will suffer sorrow.

27. The second Sajās: 232:

    You do not understand business and you will suffer regret; but there will be a gain to you, for your personal God is favourable.

28. The third Sajās: 223:

    A most serious danger to your body has passed away; your safety is solely due to the favour of the Gods.

The Three Fives (Pāñcīs)

29. The first Pāñcīs: 221

    I see that your present position is unsafe and troubled; never mind! You should undertake some business, and you shall be delivered from your misfortune.

30. The second Pāñcīs: 122:

    All regions are attacked alike; you should observe a reasonable line of conduct; otherwise you will have neither happiness or business in them at any time.

31. The third Pāñcīs: 212:

    Animal sacrifices and many other sacrifices you will sacrifice; and complete oblations you will give: there is no doubt about it.

The Three Ears (Karṇas)

32. The first Karṇas: 114:

    You will be honoured with all ceremonies; and good fortune, peace and the requisites of a King you will obtain; it will take place after a not-very-long time.

33. The second Karṇas: 141:

    By the act of God your whole property has been destroyed, ...

34. The third Karṇas: 411:

    You are contemplating a journey, but you will meet with misfortune; you will return with your business unfinished; there is no doubt about it.

The Three Shakes (Cuñcunas)

35. The first Cuncuna: 311:

    I see that after a not-very-long time you will be deprived of your pleasures: *but* you will obtain another place; do not give way to despondency.

36. The second Cuñcunas: 131:

    Wealth and perfection: these two and also family-rank, and all well-wishers; it appears you will obtain, as surely as the word of Maruta.[14]

37. The third Cuñcunas: 113:

    You are deprived of your money and forsaken by your friends and well-wishers; it appears to me as if you were troubled in your mind about relief.

The Three Makers (Karī)

38. The first Karī: 112:

    Your troubles have passed away and your misfortune likewise; you are delivered from your unlucky star; your prosperity is at hand.

39. The Second Karī: 121:

    [when] this dice-throw falls for you, you see elephants in a dream. This is a premonition of the great honour to be obtained by you, and your people, who will also be uplifted. Thoughts of prosperity, wealth and opulence, all this will come to be, nothing can prevent it, it will delight in every way.[15]

40. The Third Karī: 211:

    You dream of travelling through vast mountains, plateaux with lakes and rivers, flowers and fruits. At the end of the dream you come to a temple.This omen means you have a great deed in mind, it concerns your destiny and fortune. From this will come great pleasure and union with dear friends.[16]

The Six Abundances (Vahulas)

41. *The* first Vahula: 324:

    Long life is a great thing; you will not obtain this which is the best, *but* will obtain wealth in money and grain, and tools, and also enjoyments.

42. The second Vahula: 432:

    I see your arrival *at a place* where you have determined to go; from thence you will safely return with your goods.

43. The third Vahula: 243:

Manifold, I see, is your business and you have many friends or relations; look forward to your own happiness; you will obtain all *that belongs to it.*

44. The fourth Vahula: 423:

Manifold are your triumphs, and you have pleased your numerous friends; others will envy you; *but* you will not envy them.

45. The fifth Vahula: 342:

You are expecting a friend, and feel sure of success: *but* love is entertained reciprocally; why should he come? You should go.

46. The Sixth Vahula: 234

You are constantly worried about the wellbeing of your family, this is not uncurable, the coming of wealth well earned will quickly liberate you from your misfortune. In a dream you see a cow, a cowherd and a buffalo. Looking carefully you see water and a crossing. A difficult route through the wilderness or forest is crossed and you now understand. Pure devotion is needed, honouring the deity of your tribe (kula).

The Six Auspicious Ones (Bhādra)

47. The first Bhādra: 421:

Your disadvantages have disappeared; all your offences are forgiven; you will triumph over all your enemies; your gain is imminent.

48. The second Bhādra: 214:

In your mind you have conceived a plan for the purpose of obtaining the first place; *but* wait some time: then it will fall into your hands.

49. The third Bhādra: 142:
You will obtain a virgin, and will conciliate thy friend; the Gods will give you wealth together with affection and good luck.

50. The fourth Bhādra: 241:
You have the ability and will suffer no loss whatever; you have no cause of fear from the Gods; as you do your will[17], you will perceive your desires.

51. [Verse: The fifth Bhādra 412:] Missing
You are anxious concerning a woman, or perhaps it is a man on your mind. You have asked for wealth but you do not see any. And the pursuit of wealth has required much effort and disputations. Even so the fruits of your labours are not yet visible, and this makes you restless. Let some time pass then that good fortune will befall you.

52. The Sixth Bhādra 123
When the established person is united with a desirable partner, wealth, magical powers, well being and pursuance of inner duty is the result. On this there is no doubt. After a long time waiting this is about to happen. Knowledge of this lies in a trusted servant, do not resist it. Your mind is occupied with your predestined partner and it will be manifest in five days.

The Six Śaktīs

53. The first Śaktī: 341:

You are planning a marriage, and you will soon accomplish it, and obtain an affectionate relative who will bestow on you wealth and pleasures.

54. The second Śaktī: 134:

You are planning a meeting, and that will soon come to pass; success is ordained by the Aśvins [twin Gods of good fortune, and carved upon your skull][18] nor will it be anything unpleasant.

55. The third Śaktī: 413:

I see that something extraordinary is at hand for you and also a gain; in your household, also there will be an unequalled increase: there is no doubt about it.

56. The fourth Śaktī: 314:

As a King who has overcome all obstacles you will be well furnished with troops, conquer your enemy, and constantly rule the whole earth under your single sway.

57. The fifth Śaktī: 143:

You may not desire any friend, or you may always delight in having a friend; (but) whether you make or don't make friends, they will conceive enmity without any cause.

58. The sixth Śaktī: 431:

You are contemplating a meeting; that will certainly come to pass; in its proper time you will attain that object, and there will be no disappointment.

The Six War Drums (Dundubhis)

59. The first Dundubhi: 321:

    Whatever you have lost or has been destroyed, or stolen by thieves, or passed into other hands, that you will recover after a not-very-long time.

60. The second Dundubhi: 213:

    Whether you are forsaken by friends or whether you are supported by friends, you will obtain your desired objective, in spite of the envy of the Gods.

61. The third Dundubhi: 132:

    I see that you enjoy bodily health at the present time; from the worship of the Gods you will obtain this rest.

62. The fourth Dundubhi: 231:

    I see that you have a grievous quarrel with your enemies; but you will suffer no harm from it, and will triumph over your adversary.

63. The fifth Dundubhi: 312:

    I see that you will make a very good acquisition; moreover a boon[19] it will come to you; your wished-for desires you will obtain; there is no doubt about it.

64. The sixth Dundubhi: 124:

    You mind is much perplexed; your position is unstable; only wait one month; then you will obtain happiness.

Notes:

1 Hoernle lists one printed in 1884 in Kasi, Banares.

2 Bodl MS Sansk C.17

3 MS I: Tract on garlic and treatise on miscellaneous treatments. MS II: Navanītaka (The cream). The colophon is missing from this manuscript so the author is unknown. Hoernle dates it to 300AD. It contains extensive quotation from both Caraka and Suśruta, and other medical texts. It mentions two versions of a medical formula, an original 'thousand pepper' prescription and a shorter, more practical version that found its way into the Caraka Saṁhitā Cikitsāsthāna. The original, longer version ascribed to the Ashvins was found to be impractical.
MS III: another manual of prescriptions.
MS IV & V: two short manuals on Pāśaka-Kevalī or cubomancy. four and sixfold permutations.
MS VI & VII: various charms against snakebite.

4 Śakuna : bird, connected especially with omens. Name also of Śakuni, male relative of Gāndhāri in Mahābhārata, whose officious advice and participation in famous dice game leads to disaster. Also famous Śakuntalā, the legendary queen of ancient India, was supposedly raised by birds in the forest. The Eighteenth Century text I have used, begins 'idam pustakam shakunavali' showing how the terms dice oracle and Śakuna are synonymous.

5 This passage is written in modern Gujurati and was the appendix to one of the later manuscript of the Pāśaka-Kevalī, researched by Hoernle in the preparation of his edition of the Bower Manuscript. The translation is his.

6 Hoernle again mentions some later, Islamic manuscripts that used the six-sided dice, strong iron rods, as a form of divination. Indeed this was the form of divination known in his day and presumably survives into the present times. Divination by six sided dice was a Muslim importation and is described in a manuscript called *Ramalamrita* ; 'the fine art of Ramal' Ramal is an Arabic term for geomancy.

7 Hoernle suggest two possible translations of this phrase (Kumbhakārā-Mātanga-Yukta . 'joined with a Kumbhakārā and Mātanga'). Mātanga could refer to a man or a woman. If

female, then Mātanga women were proficient in the Magick Arts. One was employed by the emperor Āśoka's Head Queen who was jealous of her co-wife Fodhi, and wanted the Bodhi Tree to wither and afterwards revive (presumably when the co-wife went near it.) The Mātangas were described as 'dog-eaters' or outcasts. This particular Mātanga is also the name of any outcaste (chandala), perhaps the cowherdess, whom the Buddha is said to have converted. It could also be a male outcaste from the Cāṇḍālā tribe. Mātanga is also the name of an elephant, from mātam-ga (go where it wills).

8 In the Eighteenth Century text I have used to fill the lacunae in the Bower Manuscript, Matanga has become Matangini, definitely female, but with similar heterodox connections. Matangini is the daughter of Madara, King of the Vidyadharas (The possessed of science or skill). These are supernatural beings attendant on Shiva and said to be skilled in Magick. The elephant connection is still retained in the Eighteenth Century text, which begins with the following dedication 'Shriganeshaya namah.', although this is not an uncommon opening dedication.

9 This verse is incomplete.

10 The meaning is obscure. Hoernle, the original English translator suggests this as a possible meaning.

11 The wind God and considereed a luck bringer. The Tibetan luck commanding prayer-flags are generally adorned with the figure of the so-called 'wind-horse.'

12 see footnote 9.

13 The text is missing.

14 see footnote 9.

15 This verse in the Bower Manuscript is missing, I have substituted my own translation from an Eighteenth Century version of the text transcribed by Dr J.E.Schroter, Pāśaka-Kevalī - *ein indisches würfelorakel* (Borna 1900).

17 Translated from Eighteen Century manuscript.

18 original has kurvvān - duty, service.

19 actually says 'a son' but I have given this a less narrow Dundhubhi (the war drum) is one of four sons of the Asura architech Māyā.

Appendix XI
The
Hindu Lunar Calendar

The calendar, now used mainly for religious purposes is lunar, each month is a lunar month, comprised of thirty lunar days or (tithi). In some parts of India (e.g. Tamil Nadu) the month starts on the new moon, in others it is the full moon. (I use the new moon). The first fifteen days is called the bright fortnight, the next fifteen, i.e. from the full moon is called the dark fortnight.

As in Babylon an extra lunar month is inserted in the calendar every 30 months to make up the difference between the solar and lunar year. This intercalary month is added after Āṣāḍha and is called the second Āṣāḍha.

Months:

As in Ancient Egypt the new moon begins the morning after the failure to observe any trace of the waning moon. - i.e. 1st day of light fortnight/first day of lunar month

1. Caitra (Mar - Apr)
2. Vaiśākha (Apr - May)
3. Jyaiṣṭha (May - Jun)

4. Āṣāḍha (Jun - Jul)
5. Śrāvaṇa (Jul - Aug)
6. Bhādrapada (Aug - Sept)
7. Aśvina or Aśvayuja (Sept - Oct)
8. Kārttika (Oct - Nov)
9. Mārgaśīrṣa or Āgrahāyaṇa (Nov - Dec)
10. Pauṣa or Taiṣa (Dec - Jan)
11. Māgha (Jan - Feb)
12. Phālguna (Feb - Mar)

Hindu Lunar Days		Sheet Number:	
Solar Day	Translation	Lunar phase	Notes
		1	
	new crescent day	2	
	arrival day	3	
		4	
		5	
	sixth day	6	
	part day, first quarter day	7	
		8	
		9	
		10	
		11	
		12	
		13	
		14	
	half-moon day, full moon	15	

Hindu lunar days - waning fortnight		
Lunar day	Translation	Notes
16	second arrival day	
17		
18	day of the moon	
19		
20		
21		
22		
23	part day, last quarter day	
24		
25		
26		
27		
28		
29		
30		

Supplement: When your Guru Goes Gaga or when your Guru 'fails'

I have included this little piece of personal history in the hope that it might help others in their search for a spiritual teacher or at least act as a warning of the kinds of pitfall that may await. I forget the exact date of my initiation into AMOOKOS but it was some time in the early 1980s. It was at about the same time as I was being expelled from Kenneth Grant's Typhonian O.T.O. - indeed my membership of AMOOKOS was a factor in that whole affair but that's another story. Sometime in the summer of 1989 a fat envelope dropped on the mat. Amongst its enclosures was the following communication from Dadaji, the last Guru of the tiny sect of Tantrik Magi that I had joined some years earlier. What I read, with sinking heart, gave me an acute sense of déjà vu:

'Guru Purnima, Tuesday, 18th July 89
THE SPLENDOUR OF THE BRIGHT SHINING
(A Corrective to Corruption)

The International Order of Naths was founded on the desire to share my own spiritual development and Magick powers with other sincere people in the West. Having written the MSS containing the guidelines I thought that the process would develop without impediment. In this I have been wrong and inflated egos, past brainwashing and human frailty have distorted many things. I must deal with these things as individual items. I also request the editors of the *OPEN DOOR* and all other Pagan Mags to assist and make them known.

The International Order of Naths was previously known as the Western Nath Order, but as it is not exclusively for western people the name was changed to International Order of Naths (I.O.N.). The Order exists to help people to attain Enlightenment, Magick Powers, and to help to build a new amoral social order. Some groups and individuals calling themselves Cosmic People, Pagans, People of the New Aeon are all part of I.O.N. In view of my age and defects I formed a small order in the U.K. to be known as the Arcane Order of Knights of Shambhala. It was to consist of four or five of the most developed Naths in the U.K. to take over when I left this earth plane, and to direct, organize and develope the I.O.N.. Their province would be Great Britain and all Europe. The selection of anybody to AMOOKOS would first require my permission. In this way the Great Work would continue under a democratic leadership after I had gone. Every Nath or Devi must be initiated into I.O.N. by one who has already been initiated. So, in this way the transmission would go on into the New Aeon. Many Naths and Devis complained that they could not remember and some suggested an invocation to make the initiation more interesting and more colourful. This was put into writing, typed and xerox copies made. In this typed issue it was called the Prestigious Initiation into the International Order of Naths. This is the only initiation I have given and there is no other. The only addition has been the invocation which Naths have requested. I have also stressed that those who have taken the initiation without the invocation need not take it again, although many have done so.

This Nath initiation is the identical one which was given to Lalita Mataji and the same one which was given to Mike Magee. He was given this initiation and leadership of Great Britain and Europe. No other form of initiation has been given by me.

I have never initiated anyone into the Adi-Nath Sannyas Sampradaya either in India or the West. In fact, I cannot do so. To be initiated in the Adi-Nath Sampradaya one has to first renounce world, family and everything. One must not be a householder or do gainful employment or own property. This is a way of life which has existed for thousands of years. I cannot, nor would I want to break this Hindu tradition.

Some time after his initiation in the Order of Naths, Mike Magee began to republish *AZOTH*, a magazine which he had started much earlier. In the Preface of one of these issues was published the most stupid and astounding perversion of spiritual life in India and the most evil twist of any I.O.N. teaching. He claimed that I, Gurudev Mahendranath had initiated him as a sadhu and sannyasi into the Adi-Nath Sampradaya of Hindu saints. He topped this lie by stating that he was my successor and would be the Adi-Nath Guru when I died. When I wrote to Magee about this falsehood and perverted fantasy, he was most profuse in his apologies and begged me to forgive his stupid error. I promptly did so and asked him to refute this lie as soon as possible. I knew it was not a mistake but the results of his inflated ego. Now the matter has reappeared as a Nath in New York has now revealed that Magee had not only initiated him into the Adi-Nath Sampradaya but told him that he (Magee) had been given this initiation by me and that this was the only and correct initiation into the Order of Naths. It has now become most evident that my trust in Mike Magee has been badly misplaced and his object in introducing so many corruptions has been due to his inflated ego and hunger for leadership and personal power. In ten years his development and attainment towards Enlightenment has been nil and his Magick Power is still down to zero.

More than two years ago, Magee the Pagan Nath and champion for a new social order surrendered to the establishment and contracted an orthodox 'respectable' marriage at a Christian based ceremony. As the Order of Naths is Pagan and anti-establishment, Magee could no longer associate himself with the Naths or the Pagan Higher Sanctum of AMOOKOS. Gracefully he dropped out but I was deluged with letters from the U.K. asking me, 'Why has Mike dropped out?' or 'Isn't it a pity that Mike had to drop out!' I made no comment or reproach and I did not answer the questions I was asked. Evidently Mike intended and wished to continue as a personal disciple and twice sent Dakshina during the two or three years of his retirement. In March (1989) he sent me a letter with the usual apologies for his mistakes and an indication that he now wished to return to the fold and restart AMOOKOS. This was now impossible but I would agree to him rejoining I.O.N.. I want him to forget AMOOKOS for three years and concentrate on the Order of Naths. Within this three years period his domestic problem will terminate. Only then could AMOOKOS be considered. I realised also that some Naths might not recognise his return to a leading position but this could best be determined by holding a Guru or Nath fest with joy and enjoyment. I proposed he suggest that they all take initiation again and by this he could tell if the Naths were accepting him. Unfortunately he has canvassed many people about taking the initiation again but they have refused. This would indicate to me that they will not take initiation again under Mike Magee. More unfortunate is that Mike has started another panic push, terror trip and his Magic Carpet has again been snatched from underneath his feet. I can hear the laughter from here.

I am now nearing 80 years of age and the world is in turmoil. My health is in proportion to my age and eye defects require me to wear sun glasses all day and to live in a dark room. I am silent because of a defect in my speech. Magee has chosen this time to put on a big shit-stirring act and insult people, including his past Guru. These events have caused me much pain and sorrow, and Magee, whom I wanted to guide to the top has sunk to gutter level.

The Cosmos and Purusha has ways of dealing with schismatics who falsely claim Spiritual and Magick Powers. Take care lest it brings you bad luck, degeneration, and horrible rebirth. I have attained all I need to attain so please leave me in peace.
Mahendranath
Shambhala Tapovan, Mehmadabad, Gujarat, India'

'THE ULTIMATE PROMULGATION & PRONUNCIAMENTO OF H.H. SHRI GURUDEV MAHENDRANATH.

Dated Guru Pumima, 18th July in the Year 1989 A.D.

BE IT KNOWN that this day I wish to retire from all mental and physical activity of the International Order of Naths, and hereby hand over the duties of direction, instruction, and expansion to developed, loyal and noble people as follows:

THESE CHOSEN PEOPLE are the most fitted to lead the I.O.N. and the Higher Sanctum Magick Orders of MAGIKOS and AMOOKOS and their instructions and decisions are final in all matters.

Shri Kapilnath (Sir John Pilskog), I appoint as Imperator Magus Mundi to have direction of the International Order of Naths all over the world. Shri Kumari Lalita Mataji, I appoint to have authority as Imperatrix over the Naths in all the lands within the national boundaries of Canada. Shri Jadu Garudanath, I appoint as Imperator for America and to be Deputy and Helper to the Imperator Magus Mundi.

MY PREM & ASHIRVADS to all members of the International Order of Naths, and Peace, Freedom and Happiness to All.' I should say that there had been no discussion of any of these issues until this lot arrived, printed and sent from Dadaji's new man in USA. He, John Pilskog had up until then seemed a reasonable enough fellow, happy to be part of the new democratically structured East West Tantrik Order. As I say, a few years earlier I'd been expelled from Kenneth Grant's O.T.O. for various offences – perhaps even in retaliation for joining AMOOKOS! This tiny sect offered me an outlet for my interests in Indian Magick (i.e. Tantrism) and also promised to be sanctuary from the endemic infighting, egotism and strictures of the various 'Masonic' style magical orders of the time. Things in AMOOKOS were supposed to be different, and now the same things were coming up again – it was all very depressing.

Had my Guru gone gaga? Either that or he had turned into a total arsehole like every other Guru before him. Certainly over the recent years he had suffered a series of strokes the most obvious symptom of which was his current inability to write cursively (you can see examples of this on I.O.N.'s website). There were also several glaring errors of fact in the letter. The immediate one concerning Lokonath/Mike Magee, was the possible accusation of a treacherous conventional marriage by conventional Christian based ceremony. Lokanath had in fact married in 1978, just after his return from meeting Dadaji for the first time in India. It was no secret. Indeed contrary to what Dadaji says the Nath traditon is very diverse and has often included married householders. Perhaps Dadaji resented it at the time but said nothing for the ten years of highly productive work. He finally snapped in 1988, a few years before his death. The full truth will probably never be known.

As I write this circa June 2004, I am in the middle of an exchange of emails with Kapilnath (John Pilskog) the editor of *Open Door* and the person who 'benefited' most from Dadaji's *volte face.* Once upon a time I had the ultra leftist type opposition to marriage but nowadays I must say it doesn't seem that important an issue. But the fact was that Mike had married way back in 1978 and so it was hardly a recent revelation? When Mike returned from his fateful first meeting with Dadaji in the early part of 1978, he resolved to marry his longtime partner Jan, thus putting his affairs in order. I remember he said how lonely he had been during is stay in India, and that obviously influenced his decision. Perhaps when he wrote to Dadaji and told him what he'd done, he had inadvertently infringed one of Dadaji's own taboos? Even so the work continued , AMOOKOS was born and began a fitful, painfully slow growth.

Another issue was whether members of AMOOKOS could claim to be Adi-Naths. The problem started with the original charter, written in Dadaji's own inimitable style. Whatever the ambiguity of the wording, no-one claimed to be an Adinatha sannyasi. The documentary evidence shows that Lokanath certainly made no such claim. In fact, he stated that 'when my dear Gurudev Mahendranath initiated DC in India in Spring 1978, we decided to transform the tradition into an international and cosmopolitan order. This is in line with the Adinatha tradition of old, who always sought true spiritual values and repudiated the artificial.'(*AZOTH*: 13, Spring 1981). Towards the end of his life perhaps Dadaji did regret the ambiguous wording of the original charter, and, as he had done with the Uttara Kaulas, found it easier to pretend the whole thing had never happened.

It was about 1981 that I made contact with Lokanath, after buying a copy of his celebrated occult fanzine *Sothis*. Lokanath was an influential member of the UK's growing occult scene of the 1970s, and next in line to be head of the Typhonian O.T.O. What I learnt of Dadaji was from his excellent articles in *Sothis* magazine. In an important sense - Dadaji and AMOOKOS were Guru each to each.It represented a new covenant which aimed to transcend the past's inadequate magical organisations. A switch from the dominant 'Masonic' model to a more freeform 'Rosicrucian' mode. When Dadaji went gaga he forgot all this. But whatever these are the bare facts. It was never going to be clear cut. Perhaps it is a good thing that there is confusion right from the very beginning.
Yours
Mogg Morgan
(whose name in AMOOKOS is Sahajanath)

The text of Lokanath's reply

19 August 1989

Dearest Dadaji

You note that I still call you 'Dearest' because as far as I am concerned, you are still my Gurudev. You once told me that if I had any difficulties, I should just give them to you. I have done so with the current situation because I find it almost impossible to believe what is happening.

Although I really didn't want to have to do so, I am now placing on record the history of AMOOKOS and the Nathas. But first I have to deal with a statement which, according to John Pilskog, "Dadaji told me to publish." This statement is a sham, bogus, and a disgrace to the noble ideals of the Natha tradition. Mr Pilskog also told me that you had instructed him to send copies of the statement to five specific people; Dan Jacobbson, Lucien Morgan, Chris Morgan, Denny Sergeant, and Andrew Stenson. No attempt was made to send a copy of this statement to me, or to check the facts by Pilskog. When my wife, Jan Magee, told him he was responsible for the contents of this libellous rag as he was the publisher, he said to her that he disclaimed responsibility, adding that he was only doing what he was told to do by you.

I have to say that this newsletter is the most one-sided presentation and spiteful blatant propaganda that I have ever encountered in the esoteric world. And that it should emanate from the Nathas is an absolute disgrace. No opportunity is given to present the case in any kind of an objective way. What a scandal!

Aside from the gutless and sneaky way this libel was concocted, there are other issues contained in it which must be addressed. After this, I will go on to other matters which I feel every Natha should be aware of.

You make the incorrect and libellous statement that I and my wife should be shunned by all Pagans as we were married two years ago in a Christian ceremony. This is either a delusion or a lie. We were married on the 29th of December 1978 in a civil ceremony in London — nine months after I was initiated as a Natha in India.

You also appear to confuse and distort other facts — facts I may add which are backed up by documentary evidence in the shape of letters from you to me and from you to other people. For example, you make the wild clain that Lalita was initiated before me, when the documentary evidence is to the contrary. You say that I claimed to be an Adinatha sannyasi in an issue of *AZOTH*, when the documentary evidence shows that I made no such claim. In fact, I stated that 'when my dear Gurudev Mahendranath initiated DC in India in Spring 1978, we decided to transform the tradition into an international and cosmopolitan order. This is in line with the Adinatha tradition of old, who always sought true spiritual values and repudiated the artificial. *(AZOTH 13*, Spring 1981.)

This whole business of the sannyasi thing is a canard and a smokescreen. In the many editions of *Twilight Yoga* which have been published over the last ten years, you made the position of the initiation absolutely clear. You say 'All this initiation I have by initiation transmitted to Michael Magee and I have given him the Sanskrit name of Shri Lokanath as Grand Master of the New Order for the New Aeon.' *Twilight Yoga*, 1985 edition. Those who can read, can read it for themselves.

You say that I have 'stirred shit'. But it was your dictat of May 1989 stating that all Nathas had to re-undergo initiation which has actually started this terrible mess. As I wrote to you then, and as I now repeat, the vast majority of Nathas did not understand this step and refused to go for it. This is because they held what you said in your Manuscripts as sacred, viz, 'No one can take the Natha initiation away from you', 'Think for yourself' and other statements strongly advising people never to unthinkingly accept what others say. If you are now saying we all have to 'obey' — then doesn't this sharply contradict everything you have ever written and everything you have ever stood for in the past?

When I came to India in March 1978 it was not for the purpose of being some big honcho in some secret cult — as you well know. By then, I had become disillusioned with cults and orders. You, in personal conversation, made it a condition of my initiation that I attempt to spread the Nathas far and wide. I was reluctant to do so, but I agreed, and I remember clearly saying to you I was willing to do so, but I could only do it in my own way. Later, in 1980 or 1981, you encouraged and admonished me that I must start AMOOKOS, and it was your idea to start a nine degree grade system. I demurred at the time, thinking that hierarchies were squirearchies. But you insisted.

And I followed your wishes, against my own better judgement. In a letter to me you say that I should initiate candidates by post, and you drafted an application form that we adopted. It is pointless to multiply examples. But all is a matter after of record.

You have written to others and to myself alleging that AMOOKOS was corrupt. Yet you were involved in the formation of AMOOKOS at every step. You saw all the grade papers, approved of them, and I have letters from you in which you say, for example '...your fabulous MSS of AMOOKOS. well I was a little staggered by its ultra magnificence, it is really grand. New gen from old roots and it expresses your potential.' Letter dated 12/11/1980.

And in another place, 'It is now obvious to me...that the MSS have not been read or they have been read and thrown aside and the basics forgotten. It has always been my hope that some person or any persons will take these basics and rewrite them in their own individual language or argot. I don't want development and transformation to ever terminate. I do not include Lalita in this. She is an exception. She won't do anything, start anything or lead anything — either now or ever.' Letter dated January 1986.

And again, 'I leave AMOOKOS absolutely and entirely to you but will help in the background in any way you wished. Remember, although I am willing to work and spread W.N.O. in terms of numbers, AMOOKOS is your baby.' Letter dated May 1985.

In 1985, you 'excommunicated' Mr John Power, using the now familiar line that he had set himself up as a sannyasi, and that he was lying when he said that the charter you had given him was for the Uttara Kaulas. Actually, Dadaji, I have a copy of the charter you gave him somewhere or other, and you were unjust to hide. It just so happened you had given him the Uttara Kaula transmission.

As you know, I have corresponded with you over the last 13 years and have amassed a huge collection of letters which all point the opposite way from your current stance. If I had not been initiated back in March 1978, there never would have been a Natha Order, as all the people who have been initiated save one — Lalita Mataji — owe their transmission to the parampara you gave me.

You make the wild and incorrect statement that there only ever has been one initiation. This is in spite of the fact that in your manuscript 'Sinistroversus', published by Mark Bostel in 1983 in an edition of 400 copies.

I have written a very strong letter to John Pilskog demanding that the libels you write in your statement be withdrawn. I would repeat that I am ready to take action against any further slanders or libels, and will not hesitate to do so. I am not a rich person, but have the financial backing of the vast majority of the Natha community. Of course, I cannot refute any allegations you make about my attainment and the like. After all, what difference can there be between one rat-race and any other? Who is doing the judging?

And the matter of dakshina Jan and I have sent to you is between us and you. But we sent you £25 every month, without fail, for four years. When I lost my job, you told me to send money only when we could afford it. We gave birth to our beautiful boy Tamlin, and I found myself a new and demanding job. How then can you use this question of dakshina as a matter of contention?

But what I can say is that I have fearlessly struggled to maintain the unity of the Natha community, and have withheld nothing of this affair from anyone I have talked to.

Now that you have issued this statement, it seems to me the situation is virtually unretrievable between us. But I am writing this letter in one last, probably vain attempt, to preserve the unity of our Order.

You blacken my name by making out that I have somehow constantly apologised for my mistakes. Well, I do admit mistakes have been made. And when I have made then, I have not sought to pass the buck. I am not ashamed to apologise. No stigma is attached to it in my eyes.

Can we not bury this black business and get back to some sort of reality? I have still not lost my ideals and the hope that this situation can somehow be rescued from the jaws of dismal factionalism.

You close the statement that Pilskog alleges you ordered him to distribute by issuing a veiled threat that schismatics might be doomed to further rebirth as lower life forms. But at our Guru Purnima in Oxford in July 1989 we rejected schism outright as an option. The Natha Community and AMOOKOS are healthy, stable and free organisations. We do not want schism. The question that all Nathas worldwide are asking of you. Why are you pursuing this matter which contradicts all you have ever written and said in the past? If the dictat is that we must obey questioningly, I fear you will only be left with 'yes men' and 'yes Devis'. Do you really want this to happen? My own feeling is that this is all a terrible, bloody shame, a waste of energy, and a great, great pity. Cannot we end it now? Pilskog's statement has been sent, so he says, to five people, and I must copy this letter to them and to him. I must also send a copy to faithful Shyamanatha in New York, and to Doc Sandy Indradhanush in Nairn.

Your ever devoted

Lokanath

No names, no pack drill.

cc: DS, A S, J P, DJ, SM, LM, CM, JE

Final comment from Sahajanath

Lokanath was wasting his time really - the decision had already been made and Dadaji was locked into his position. I'm really glad I did not allow myself to get as close to Dadaji as he did. The people who benefited from Dadaji's madness were also unwilling to see sense. Just before his death Dadaji decided that he must will his intellectual property to these same people. So a once intelligent Mahatma who has taken vows never to own property has suddenly decided he had some. The 'failure' or 'failing' of the Guru may be something we should consider as built into the Nath tradition. The more sanguine might say it's built into the human condition - even the powers of the Buddha declined towards the end. Matsyendranath, the founder of the Kaula practice, abandoned his role as Guru in order to retire to a sensual earthly paradise. He was succeeded by Gorakhnath, who then extended and built upon what Matsyendranath had begun. This unstable condition of 'permanent revolution' is natural.

In 2004, I wrote to the I.N.O. in their role of literary executors asking for permission to reproduce some of Dadaji's works. They were still locked into the old conflict and would not allow it. There have been moments when it seemed possible to reframe this whole thing and reunite but they always come to nothing. It's time to move on. The truth is that Dadaji's works, interesting as they can sometimes be, are far from the final word. It would be nice to keep them alive but events make the easiest road that of creating something new, doing some fresh research of our own, making up our own ideas. The scarey sounding phrase 'Kill the Guru' actually means to move beyond mortal teachers. In the case of our Nath tradition, the Guru in effect 'killed' himself.

PS: Do please check out the I.N.O. website (www.mahendranath.org) for their version of the facts.

Summer 1 Volume 2 No. 2 1989

NEWSLETTER OF THE INTERNATIONAL ORDER OF NATHS AND FRIENDS

SKULL CHATTER

Greetings and welcome to an unusual edition of *THE OPEN DOOR*. Our Summer edition was delayed for printing while we waited for some news relating to an organizational controversy which had regretably arisen. Our expectations and delay proved to be justified as we recently received two envelopes from Shree Gurudev Mahendranath containing the facts and documentation on this matter.

In the first envelope was a MS entitled: 'THE SPLENDOR OF THE BRIGHT SHINING (A Corrective to Corruption)' This MS is now typeset and presented as the major offering and conversation piece for this issue. Due to the nature and serious statements contained in this MS our legal counsel advised us to include a reduced xerox copy of Shree Mahendranath's original MS as an insert. This exhibit A was included in order to prove the authenticity of the document and to also eliminate any possible suspicion that the MS was victimized by editorial hyperbole or corruption. The second envelope we received contained Mike Magee's (Lokanath) latest aerogram to Shree Gurudev and also a statement issued by Shyamanatha of Sacred Stone Nation zonule, New York

City. These two documents have been reduced and included on the flip side of the insert as exhibit B. We felt it was important to include these two items on the insert as they both contain information which is referred to in Shree Gurudev's MS and may also be of interest to those who have little knowledge of the confusion and its degree of seriousness. At this point I wish to apologize and beg the indulgence of our greater public who may be less than thrilled by our public exhibition of house cleaning and garden weeding. Since this matter is of great importance for the future of our Nath Order we felt obligated to devote this edition to its clarification. We hope you all can be good sports about this and perhaps derive some amusement from the excitement and historical significance of the information. Most other news items now pale in comparison to recent events so we will devote this entire issue to the matter at hand. It is our wish that the machinations which have led up to this situation and ensuing clarification be put behind us, and that a time of clarity and understanding will follow. Please read on with care and think about these things. – Kapilnath

The newsletter contained the following editorial:
EDITORIAL

Sadly, the production and mailing of this edition of *THE OPEN DOOR* has been a task devoid of joy. The very fact that situations have occurred which culminated in our beloved Gurudev Mahendranath having to issue a clarification subtitled

(A Corrective to Corruption) is an event which has saddened me greatly. After lengthly discussions with fellow zonule members and others, a decision was made to organize and format the newsletter in the manner it is now presented. We all felt the documentation provided is adequate to bring the matter fully to light and eliminate the possibility of future obfuscations or misinterpretations. I feel the material speaks for itself, and for this reason we have added no commentary on the matter. It is the wish of Shree Gurudev that his MS be made known to the Nath community. For this reason it will be mailed to those of you who have been in touch with our zonule regardless of whether or not you have subscribed. This is our last exception. I encourage all who wish to remain informed to subscribe today. Yearly rates for 4 issues are $5 domestic and $6 for overseas orders. Those who are interested can contact our mailing address. Now is the time to put this matter behind us and use our resources to construct a Bright and Shining future. My Best Wishes to you All.

Kapilnath

INTERNATIONAL ORDER OF NATHS

Index

E

F

G

H

I

J

K

L

M

N

O

P

Q

R

S

Mandrake

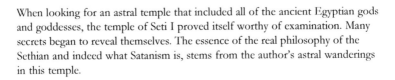

Other Related Titles of Interest

Tankhem:
Seth & Egyptian Magick Vol I
By Mogg Morgan
£12.99, isbn 978-1869928865, 234pp,
second revised edition

The Typhonian deity Seth was once worshipped in Ancient Egypt. Followers of later schools obliterated Seth's monuments, demonised and neglected his cult. A possible starting point in the quest for the 'hidden god' is an examination of the life of Egyptian King Seti I ('He of Seth') also known as Sethos.

When looking for an astral temple that included all of the ancient Egyptian gods and goddesses, the temple of Seti I proved itself worthy of examination. Many secrets began to reveal themselves. The essence of the real philosophy of the Sethian and indeed what Satanism is, stems from the author's astral wanderings in this temple.

The temple is a real place, and like any temple no part of its design is accidental. It is a record in stone and paint of the Egyptian wisdom. It also fits quite well with the Thelemic mythos and tells lots of interesting things about the ancient Seth cult - if you have the eye to see it.

Contents: Prolegomena to Egyptian magick; Setanism; Tankhem; Egyptian Magick and Tantra; Sexual Magick; Twenty Eight; North; The Crooked Wand.

The author has published numerous articles, short stories and books, principally Ayurveda: Medicine of the Gods, The English Mahatma (a Tankhem novel) and as ('Katon Shual') Sexual Magick.

A complementary ebook (*House of Life*) with an introductory magical practice is available with the above title on request.

For these & other titles contact:
Mogg Morgan, (01865) 243671
mandrake@mandrake.uk.net
web: mandrake.uk.net
PO Box 250, Oxford, OX1 1AP (UK)

Lightning Source UK Ltd.
Milton Keynes UK

173656UK00001B/45/P

9 781869 928421